THE BUTCHER'S GUIDE TO WELL-RAISED MEAT

HOW TO BUY, CUT, AND COOK GREAT BEEF, LAMB, PORK, POULTRY, AND MORE

JOSHUA and JESSICA APPLESTONE
of Fleisher's Grass-Fed & Organic Meats,
and ALEXANDRA ZISSU

Clarkson Potter/Publishers
New York

Copyright © 2011 by Joshua Applestone, Jessica Applestone,
and Alexandra Zissu
Photographs copyright © 2011 by Jennifer May
Illustrations copyright © 2011 by Gunar Skillins

Published in the United States by Clarkson Potter/
Publishers, an imprint of the Crown Publishing Group,
a division of Random House, Inc., New York.
www.crownpublishing.com
www.clarksonpotter.com

CLARKSON POTTER is a trademark and POTTER with
colophon is a registered trademark of Random House, Inc.

Library of Congress Cataloging-in-Publication Data
Applestone, Joshua.
The butcher's guide to well-raised meat: how to buy, cut,
and cook great beef, lamb, pork, poultry, and more /
Joshua Applestone, Jessica Applestone, Alexandra Zissu.
    p. cm.
1. Meat. 2. Meat cuts. 3. Cooking (Meat) I. Applestone,
Jessica. II. Zissu, Alexandra. III. Title.

TX373.A67 2011
641.6'6—dc22   2010042079

ISBN 978-0-307-71662-0
eISBN 978-0-307-95338-4

Printed in the United States of America

Design by Marysarah Quinn

Insert photographs (insert page 10, bottom left;
insert page 11, middle right) by Dietrich Gehring

10 9 8 7 6 5 4 3 2 1

First Edition

We dedicate this book to the farmers and their animals
who make our work possible.

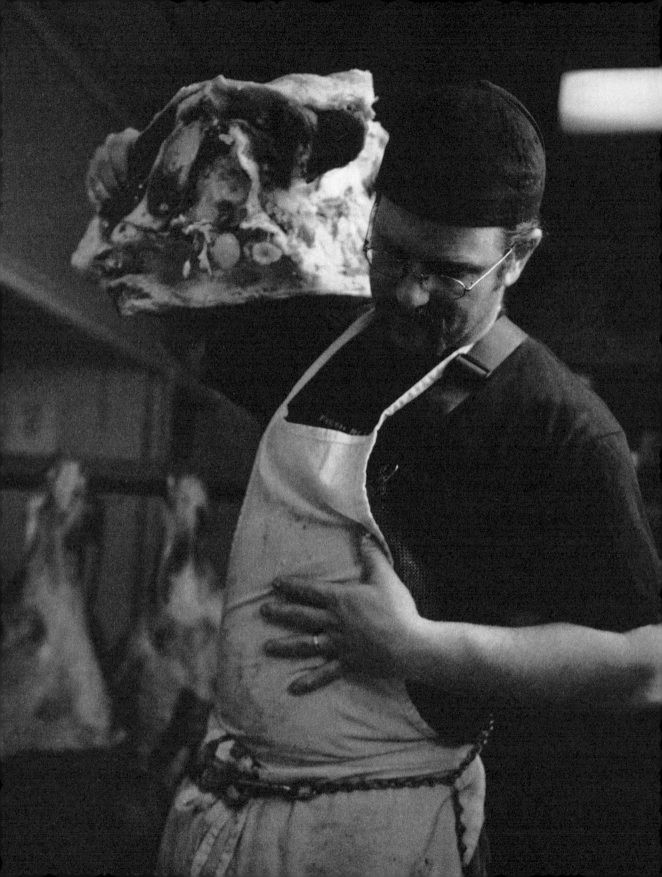

PREFACE

TRY TO CONJURE UP AN IMAGE OF A BUTCHER IN YOUR MIND. You're not alone if you can't. Most Americans don't interact with butchers much these days. They are a dying breed. You probably don't even have a butcher shop in your town anymore. There might be a guy in a bloody apron lurking behind the scenes at your supermarket, but he rarely makes an appearance near the refrigerated displays of shrink-wrapped boneless skinless chicken breasts. The people who deal with boxed or industrially processed meats are not butchers. They have no skills. All they have to do is open a bag, drain the blood, and hand it to the customer. They're just clerks with a propensity for knives.

It used to be that every town had a butcher and in most there were two or three. The butcher shop was the place you visited weekly, or even daily, to pick up meat or gossip with the guy behind the counter—who was probably the son of the guy your mother gossiped with. This was the place where you got your Sunday dinner, your fresh ground for meat loaf, your holiday roast. The place where you could ask for a particular cut and after the first few times have it become your regular order. The place where the butcher leaned across the counter with a slice of bologna for your child. Even if you don't actually remember any of that, you do. It's part of our collective unconscious.

This was the type of place that in the spring of 2004 my wife, Jessica, and I set out to open. An old-school butcher shop with a modern-day twist—sourcing and selling only grass-fed and organic meat. We returned to the nearly lost tradition of buying and carving whole animals—all of them humanely raised on pasture, never administered hormones or antibiotics, and slaughtered at small local facilities near the farms they roam on, close to our shop in New York's Hudson Valley. From birth to when they become meat in our cases, these animals have been touched by only a few sets of hands: the farmer's, the slaughterer's, and ours. We know where they have been every step of the way.

The story of how we founded our shop sounds like the setup to a bad joke: "So a vegan and a sometime vegetarian decide to open a butcher shop . . ." Laugh all you like but it's true—when we started I was a devoted vegan of sixteen years and Jessica was a vegetarian (with a bacon exception). But it wasn't quite as strange as it seems. I come from a long line of butchers, which skipped my parents' generation. I got into the family trade after I went to college, then spent fifteen years as a chef. When I met Jessica, she had toyed with vegetarianism off and on. Around then she decided to return to eating meat, but only from ethically raised animals, not the stuff from your average supermarket. She had become deeply immersed in research on pastured animals in her quest to eat sustainable local meat. Jessica is a label reader but even she had

trouble deciphering what she was finding. One of our supermarkets slapped "Local" stickers on their beef. Did that mean that the animals were pastured and raised without hormones or antibiotics? When she asked, no one at the store knew the answer. Some larger natural supermarkets had policies and standards that they were supposed to adhere to, but when she questioned their employees, they either knew nothing or offered contradictory information, and sometimes the meat they claimed to sell wasn't on the shelves in the stores near us. She turned to online shopping. Unfortunately the websites touting grass-fed product were not only hard to verify but sold frozen meat shipped from the Midwest. Jessica was frustrated and confused. She started exploring the option of buying a whole animal directly from a local farmer—the only way she had come across of really knowing how and where it had been raised—but the idea was overwhelming; after all, she was the only one eating meat in our home. One day she lamented that she didn't want to buy a whole steer for one grass-fed steak. Her dream was a butcher shop where she could walk in, buy a well-raised rib eye, talk to the butcher about where it came from and how to cook it, and walk out. I couldn't believe no one was purchasing whole local animals, breaking them down, and selling them. So we set about opening exactly what Jessica

have customers who have turned into life-long friends. And how could they not? We see them every week, more often than our own families most of the time. We are an integral part of their lives and they ours. We know when there is a baby on the way or when there has been a divorce (usually we get the wife when they split), when there is an illness in the family (more prepared foods) or even a death. We kvell as we watch kids who were in their mommas' bellies when we first opened now asking for a rotisserie chicken wing. And they rejoiced with us when our child was born.

Even the physical space harkens back to a pre-supermarket time when butcher shops were the norm. Our shelves are wooden and lined with local and organic dry goods. A butcher block belonging to my great-grandfather, Wolf Fleisher, is proudly displayed, and our entryway is lit by the same light he had hanging in his Brooklyn shop—the original Fleisher's. Our floors are iconic black-and-white checkerboard and our name out front is emblazoned in the same scripted gold leaf Wolf had above his door. The only thing missing is the sawdust.

No one is going to get rich running a butcher shop, but our philosophy of sustainability has kept us going. As our former apprentice and friend Julie Powell described it in *Cleaving: A Story of Marriage, Meat, and Obsession,* the book she wrote based partially on her time at Fleisher's,

wanted. Her desire for easy access to a small amount—not a year's supply—of sustainably raised meat that was fresh, not frozen, and custom-cut resulted in Fleisher's Grass-Fed & Organic Meats. We run the shop together; we are partners in every sense. Applestone, by the way, is her last name. Fleisher is my family name. And yes, we know it means butcher; that's the point.

Jessica likes to call Fleisher's the "Cheers" of butcher shops. It's a place where everybody knows your name or at least your favorite cut. It has happily become a community gathering spot. We

"It might be a neighborhood butcher shop, or it might be a political movement masquerading as a neighborhood butcher shop." It's both. We write in the manual we give new employees that the act of eating is inherently a political one. Though we didn't come up with that idea, we realize that every bite of food we consume affects the animal from which it came, the farmer who raised that animal, the environment, and our health. Our staff at this point literally roll their eyes every time they hear us say it, but we never forget that animals die for our business and your dinner. So, we do our best to honor these animals and the farmers who raise them. Fleisher's exists so people can come and feel good about what they eat and we can feel good about what we sell. When we started, ours was one of the only butcher shops in the nation specializing in sustainable butchery. Even though cutting whole animals is what all butchers used to do every day, almost no one does this anymore. Butchery was always a valid trade, then a lost art, so now it's exotic, unknown.

Through the years we have watched people's lives change—ours included—as they have become part of the sustainable movement. Vegans have become omnivores; families have started to shop, cook, and garden together; and farmers' markets have become the new town square. People have begun to understand more about their food—how it was raised and where it comes from. They're responding to the provenance as well as the flavor, and are inspired to learn more. That's what we want, that's what we strive for at the shop. With *The Butcher's Guide to Well-Raised Meat*, we're thrilled to bring this education beyond our doors. An army of well-informed consumers has a unique ability to further impact our food system. We are offering up the whole picture—from farm to slaughterhouse to butcher block to plate—to empower everyone to make informed choices no matter where they live or shop. And we have crammed the following pages with insider information, advice, encouragement, and practical tips to help the process. We hope it will become your trusted guide to sourcing, cutting, cooking, and enjoying good meat.

We never forget that animals die for our business and your dinner.

OUR STORY

FOUNDING FLEISHER'S WAS CHAOS. I'm a leap-then-look kind of guy, but I should have looked more first. Hindsight. We signed a lease on a space around the corner from our current location before we found sources for meat or lined up the slaughterhouse—in other words, totally backward and not something we would advise anyone to do. But overcoming these considerable obstacles was an amazing education. Nowadays we happily consult with people interested in opening sustainable butcher shops so they don't make the same mistakes we did. Our learning curve was not a curve at all; it literally went straight up and we've never stopped learning. We had to educate ourselves on not just butchery but also animal husbandry, sustainable farming, and slaughtering practices. We got up to speed on everything from the use of hormones and antibiotics in animals to carbon sequestration to seasonal concerns affecting Hudson Valley farms to sourcing local cheese, dairy, and eggs (we sell all three). We needed to learn to ask the right questions of our farmers and slaughterhouse owners. In time these questions became our standards. We had to figure out how to sell to retail customers and how to educate our wholesale restaurant customers about what we were doing. We needed to become expert charcuterie makers. It was all new territory for us, and as far as we knew there was nobody in the country doing what we were doing. Factor in that we chose to do this at a time when butcher shops were drastically in decline in America, and in a depressed upstate New York town. It's a wonder that we made it, but here we are.

Before we opened, neither of us had ever broken down a whole animal. I have butchery in my blood, had carved meat as a chef, and thought I knew a lot more than I did. Technically I'm a third-generation butcher. My grandfather, Jack, and great-grandfather, Wolf, both owned and operated Fleisher's Meats in Windsor Terrace, Brooklyn. The shop closed when I was a kid, but it was formative. Wolf was nearly ninety when I knew him, but I still remember him as a real butcher, a real meat man. Jack was a huge presence in my life and was alive until just before I turned thirty. Pictures from the shop and his old butcher blocks were in my home when I was growing up. Jack was knowledgeable about food and loved to eat. He was also an artist—we have his gorgeous burnished wood sculptures in our home—and explained how meat is art, that whatever you do is an expression of art. He always said to be a really good butcher you needed to be someone who has experienced life and can turn that into a sellable product. You have to know opera and how to cook, and remember everything about the customer. I think what my grandfather meant was that it takes a well-rounded human being to be able to *kibitz* with customers. It was opera and the Dodgers in his day and politics and the Mets in mine. Most customers have a romantic notion of what a butcher is. They come and they want a little philosophy with their brisket, a few jokes with their chops. They want to make that connection, and I know that they would be happier with a butcher who was a failed poet than with a guy who stands behind the counter and just cuts meat for a living. If that's all they wanted, they could hit the intercom at any supermarket. It's why they come to a butcher shop.

FLEISHER'S GRASS-FED
& ORGANIC MEATS
- All Pastured Raised to
100% Grass-Fed
- All Local
- Everything
No Antibiotics
No Hormones
No Pesticides
-CHICKEN 100% Certified Organic
PLEASE ASK IF YOU DON'T SEE
WHAT YOU WANT
NOW FLEISHER'S DOES
WWW.FL
POT PIES
MEATBALLS
HOT DOGS
FLEISHER'S
STOCKS
And Don't
LIVE
.C
DAYTON

Many warned us we couldn't succeed; it wasn't the way of the world anymore.

Sadly my grandfather wasn't around to advise me when we were deciding to open Fleisher's. So Jessica and I went in search of old-time butchers and asked for their help. Some of these guys continue to assist us today. Their grandsons aren't butchers, their family butcher shops are closed, and we're grateful they have been happy to share their wisdom with us. Not that all the old-timers were cheerleaders. Many warned us we couldn't succeed; it wasn't the way of the world anymore. Americans are no longer accustomed to walking into a butcher shop and asking for cuts and cooking advice. Some told me we would eventually fail. No one ever wanted to talk in front of Jessica. They would drink coffee and walk around the block with me. One pulled me close: "You have a beautiful wife. You want to *lose* her? Because you're going to have to close your doors. I'll help you, but you're *not* going to make it." They helped us out of pity more than anything else. We understood that this was a long shot, that no one else was doing what we wanted to do. But we were hell-bent on trying to change how people eat, how they shop. We *knew* it was a great idea. So we picked up as much wisdom as

these guys were willing to provide. They were essential in teaching me the basics, from butchering whole animals to setting up a case. They all have their own tricks of the trade. They have taught us to use gravity as we table-break, or bench-break, for example, rather than brute force. A quick push on top of a joint lying off the table does in seconds what a knife would do in minutes. All you need is some leverage and a thrust. Where else could I have learned these skills that had already become an almost forgotten memory to most?

It's ironic that one of our most important mentors had had a family butcher shop himself right around the corner from Fleisher's. Schneller's was famous in the area for its prime meat and home-made sausages, and Tom Schneller had grown up behind that counter. Schneller's had closed some years before (we had even considered the space when we were looking to open Fleisher's), but its reputation remained. To this day when we mention that we have a butcher shop in Kingston, New York, old-time locals immediately assume it *is* Schneller's. About a year after we opened, Tom himself, a Culinary Institute of America meat fabrication instructor, walked into our shop and offered to show me the ropes. I breathed a huge sigh of relief and said, "We don't know what the hell we're doing. I know we could be doing this better." Now we do, thanks to Tom and so many other guys who have helped us keep a dying art—and ourselves—alive.

Jess started out cutting with me. Eventually we divided the labor. I focused on everything with four legs, and Jess turned her attention to everything with two. She's responsible for making sure our name gets out there, staff training, customer service (not my strong suit), finding incredible sources of local cheese and dairy, and rolling her eyes every time I come up with another "great" idea.

Beyond learning to carve, my job was to go out and find farmers, to source, and to go to slaughterhouses. We knew we

were looking for the cleanest and safest producers and slaughterhouses we could find, but safety is subjective. We don't believe that it's safe to irradiate your meat, dye it, fill it with antibiotics, hormones, and preservatives. We find it unnerving that the United States Department of Agriculture (USDA) regulates how many rat droppings can be in our food but somehow these rules don't put a dent in the massive food recalls that seem to happen every month. We decided that for us safety would be about trust and small-scale producers, small farmers, small slaughterhouses, local community. When I found the names of farmers, we would drive over to their farms. We quickly realized we knew nothing about farming. One of the best farmers we ever met taught me that when you go on a farm you have to look at the grass and know the earth it springs from. Look at what the animals are eating—this will tell you what's truly going on. A good cattle farmer is really a grass farmer. To get the right nutrients, the animals should rotate from pasture to pasture, naturally weed-whacking as they go but not overgrazing. Overgrazing leads to soil erosion and runoff. Healthy grass from well-rotated pastures can absorb carbon. We had no idea.

We found that the small farmers most likely to be raising their animals well and on good feed aren't at it full-time. To make ends meet, they have to work day

jobs and tend to the animals in the morning and at night. The fictional Farmer John and Mrs. John taking care of the homestead was just that—fiction. We also thought we would find farmers who were reading the same books Jess was dog-earing, the sort of people you might meet in a farmers' market who left a city to *get back to the land*. And we did—and some were great farmers—but many were in the same position we were: at the bottom of a very steep learning curve. Real farmers for the most part—and I'm overgeneralizing here but bear with me—don't have dog-eared copies of Michael Pollan's books on their bedside tables. They're not sending in contributions to the Natural Resources Defense Council. And they're not particularly interested in having a bunch of sustainable agriculture groupies traipsing around on their land every weekend while they're trying to work. There are exceptions to this, of course—the rancher and author Bill Niman and the grass farmer, author, *Food, Inc.* star, and one of our heroes Joel Salatin both come to mind. But generally speaking, farmers are farmers. They work really hard. And that work isn't political. Our farmers raise animals well and don't abuse them or their land because that's the best practice. Maybe they've heard of Slow Food or read *Fast Food Nation* and maybe they haven't. If they're angry about our messed-up food system, it's the part that pertains to them—the small-family-versus-large-corporate-farms issue, or the government regulations that often crush them. We have found that knowing we only sell grass-fed and organic meat doesn't really matter to them. Sometimes it does a little, but mainly what matters is that they get paid. Consistently. We pay 15 to 25 percent more than market rate. Without us, they usually have to sell the animals at auction and take whatever is offered. What we do allows them to do what they do.

Thankfully our days of wandering around random farms didn't last long, because we happened on local meat fixture Ted Johnson, a butcher/slaughterer/middleman. He hooked us up with meat and, most important, a small local slaughterhouse. They are the necessary link between sustainable farmer and local butcher, and yet there aren't enough of them out there (for more on slaughterhouses, see page 40). Jessica claims Ted took us under his wing and taught us everything he knew because I called him for the first time at 6:30 a.m.—non-city-slicker time. I don't think I had been to

bed yet. We were strange bedfellows. Actually most of the people we work with are—they respect us and support us and we respect them and support them. We just can't talk about politics or religion. What we have in common matters more. As far as Ted was concerned, we had wildly unrealistic ideas of how animals should be raised. Still, he was patient with us and promised that he would find animals that had never been given "the juice," as he called hormones and antibiotics. While we waited for his call, we painted the store and prepared to open.

This was March 2004. When Ted called, he wanted me to come and meet one of our future farmers in Massachusetts, less than two hours from our Kingston shop. Although I had spent considerable time around meat as a chef, I hadn't spent much time on farms. Jess kept joking about how neither one of us had ever been on a farm besides the Long Island Game Farm growing up. I dressed wrong for the freezing weather in jeans and a T-shirt. I wore sneakers. Now we know you do not step out of your car on a farm without boots. March means mud and the farm was covered in it—and shit—knee-deep.

Look at what the animals are eating—this will tell you what's truly going on. A good cattle farmer is really a grass farmer.

WHAT WE EXPECT FROM OUR FARMERS

❖ Animals must come from local farms (within a 150-mile radius).

❖ Animals must be raised on the farm from birth to death or must be bought from a small local farm that specializes in birthing animals, like a cow/calf operation. (Small farmers tend to breed pigs and lambs where they are raised and "finished"—fattened for slaughter.)

❖ Animals must *never* be given antibiotics or hormones—not just taken off drugs for a period of time and tested "clean" before slaughter.

❖ If an animal is bought at auction, the farmer must provide paperwork proving that the animal has *never* been given antibiotics or hormones, and the animal must be from a reputable farm.

❖ Animals may be treated with antibiotics for illness but then must be removed from the herd and sold to a different purchaser.

❖ Animals must be fully pastured—we call this pasture-raised. Ruminants (animals with four-compartment stomachs designed to digest grasses) must have access to grass or hay throughout their lives. To us, *fully pastured* means animals are outside on pasture 100 percent of the time, but it does not have to mean that their diet consists only of grass. If it does, that's called 100 percent grass-fed, or grass-fed/grass-finished; see page 228)

❖ Animals may be grass-fed/grain-finished or 100 percent grass-fed if ruminants.

❖ Animals may be fed grain either grown on the farmer's land or purchased from a local co-op. Grain must be free of pesticides and herbicides; organic is preferred but is more often than not prohibitively expensive for small farmers.

❖ Animals must be processed at a nearby slaughterhouse and can never travel more than a couple of hours to get to one. Travel is stressful for animals.

WHAT'S IN A NAME

You might have already noticed that despite the fact that every menu in America seems to list farm names these days, and customers really like—and ask for—farm names, we don't name-drop, and you won't find farm names on labels sticking out of the meat in our cases. The main reason we don't name names is that they can be misleading. There's a misguided sentiment among consumers that if meat comes from a farm with a name, it's automatically good—pastured, raised without the use of hormones and antibiotics, humane. But that's just not true. A name doesn't tell you anything about the farmer or the farming methods. Heard of Shady Brook Farms? Does that bucolic name trigger trust, make you feel like animals raised there must be treated well? Sorry, but Shady Brook is owned by the agribusiness giant Cargill Meat Solutions Corporation. If they're hip to the farm name game, we don't want to be.

When people ask us if we know such-and-such farm, chances are we don't. While we're lucky enough to live in the Hudson Valley where there are many, many farms, most of these are small—they slaughter, like, three steers a year. That wouldn't last us a week. We spend a lot of our time researching and thinking about farms, and yet we can't possibly know the names of all of them. Besides, many of our farmers don't use names. They're working farmers who don't have the legacy of naming their farms. It's just what they *do*. One of our slaughterhouse guys raises animals for us on his land. There's no name for that. It's just Mike's place. Know it? No. Of course you don't—you shouldn't! Most of our farms don't sell to anyone but Fleisher's, so their names wouldn't mean anything to anyone but us. So the next time you see a farm name, please ask the butcher, store manager, or waiter what it means—where it is, what sort of farming they do, who owns them—before you bite.

Ted and the farmer, correctly dressed, were in the field next to hulking Black Angus steers, which can weigh well over 1,000 pounds. They told me to come on out, so I waded in and watched as they slapped an enormous creature on the ass, showing me the proper way to check if a steer is ready for market. If the aitchbone, its haunches, is too bony or visible, it's not. Shivering, I spied a steer across the field in a hut with a fence around it. I was mainly keeping my mouth shut so I wouldn't seem like the novice I was, but I couldn't help but ask, "What's with the cow over there? Is it sick?" Let me give you a little tip: If you find yourself on a farm trying to look like you know what you're doing, remember, a *cow* is only ever female, a bull has balls, and a steer is castrated. Cows are for milk; steers are for steak. The farmer explained that he had had to become a four-season farm to support himself—adding U-pick strawberries, sleigh rides, and a petting zoo. The steer with the house was the farm's mascot. It would never be slaughtered. Oddly its name was Speckles, not Lucky.

The farmer offered me a sample to take home. I left out the part about being a vegan, thanked him, and took a skirt steak to cook for Jess. She proclaimed it a complete and total revelation, like nothing she had ever had before: delicious, kind of livery. When Ted heard that, he instructed us *never* to use the word *livery*

in front of a customer. But she meant it in a good way—earthy, grassy, animaly, *flavorful*. So we had beef for the shop. We were on our way. Ted helped connect us to other farmers who raised pigs and lambs. We started to understand what we had to offer farmers: a guarantee. We were prepared to pay steadily and year-round. If they sold to us, they didn't need to deal with farmers' markets or do any of their own marketing.

Our role in this system quickly grew clearer. As Jessica likes to say, "We don't sell meat; we sell trust." Over the years we have seen that Fleisher's attracts three types of customers and we love all of them. We've got the philosophical types—locavores who want nothing more than to support the local economy and who are very concerned about environmental impact and the welfare of the farmer and his animals. We see our fair share of health-conscious people seeking out grass-fed meat because it's said to contain more nutrients and fewer toxins than factory-farmed grain-fed meat. Often they have beaten cancer, or they're trying to feed the right thing to their young children. Our foodie customers don't tend to care where the meat comes from or what nutrients it might contain; they are here for the flavor. We had been focused on sourcing well-raised animals but always remembered to put flavor right up there in terms of importance. You can sell anything

WHAT WE CARRY

We decided to keep our offerings narrow and to do them well. No ostrich, no emu, no alligator. No cases full of charcuterie. Just beef, lamb, pork, chicken, fresh sausages. Turkey for holidays. Sometimes veal and duck. Infrequently customers have special-ordered goat. And, even less frequently, they ask for offal, which, being a whole animal operation, we have plenty of. We would love to have even more adventurous customers interested in sustainable options. But generally speaking it's the rare person who walks in the shop looking for tripe, tongue, or even rabbit. We recognize that Americans want it all in one place. So we conceded by offering pretty much all you'd ever need to make dinner. We have stock, a lovingly curated selection of regional/East Coast artisanal cheeses, local milk, yogurt, and pastured eggs, some dried beans, grains, a few bottles of oil, and the occasional local vegetable, including onions. If you need inspiration, we have some books on hand. We even have soap handcrafted from our beef tallow.

once, but if it doesn't taste good, the customer won't come back.

It was complicated when we opened the store and I was cutting but not tasting. Jess really felt that if we were selling it, I had to eat it. There were some difficult moments because we never told anyone I was a vegan—I remember one particularly awkward tasting meal at Blue Hill at Stone Barns with chef Dan Barber. But Jess didn't have to push hard. I *was* curious. Our bacon put me over the edge six months after we opened shop. (Hence the line on our best-selling T-shirt: BACON: THE GATEWAY MEAT.) Shortly after that I was eating everything else, too. I felt that good about its origins and its treatment.

Fleisher's has been a learning process on every level. Finding farmers who do what we want consistently, and with

EATING ANIMALS

Now we refer to ourselves as ethical carnivores and know plenty of other vegetarians who have made the switch to pasture-raised and organic meat. Obviously there's a difference between vegans and vegetarians. If you are not eating animal by-products at all, that's one thing—you have effectively taken yourself out of the system. But we are always baffled by the e-mails we get protesting what we do from vegetarians who eat conventional dairy and eggs. If you put cheese from the worst-treated cows imaginable on your (decidedly un-local) veggie burgers, we have a hard time entering into a discussion with you. If your cheese and eggs come from the kinds of animals we sell, great, let's talk. But it's the rare vegetarian who eats that way.

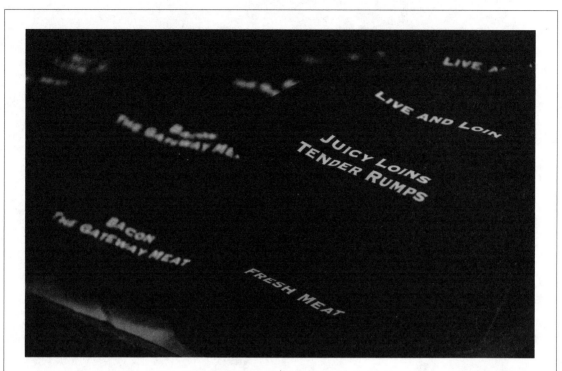

enough livestock to sell to us, took time, trial and error, and persistence. Finding and keeping customers has been another challenge. Many people didn't get it that our prices reflect the true cost of food in an arena dominated by industrial product loaded with subsidized corn and soy. The expense of hand-raising animals—locally raised grains, fuel oil—is astronomical. The operating costs are all through the roof. You would think subsidies might help here, too, but a disproportionate percentage of the money our government pays farmers to grow our food goes to the big corporate operations, and small farmers doing things right struggle.

But we have seen a change. Since 2004, our customers are starting to get it more and more. And demand is growing. They know something about sustainability, and are beginning to understand that every part of the system needs to be sustainable—the farmer, the slaughterhouse, the butcher, the feed, the transportation, the waste management, and even the cuts of meat—not just the animals.

Along the way, there were so many times when we almost had to close our doors. Each time, one or the other of us would beg, plead, or cajole to try again, just stay open to Thanksgiving, Christmas, or the Fourth of July. The thing that always kept us going was the community and the thought that we could change the world one chicken leg at a time.

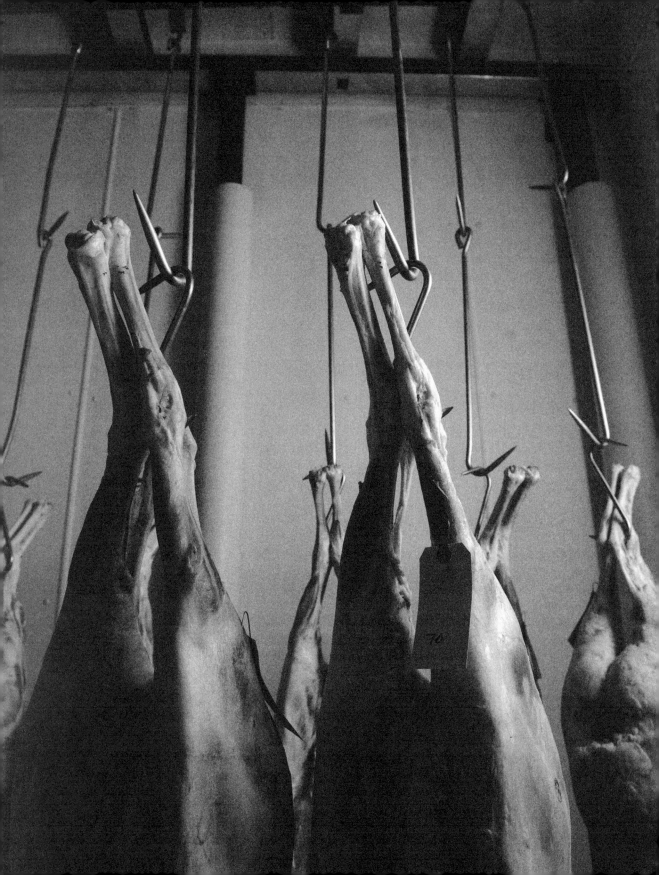

THE
BACKSTORY

WE'RE NOT HISTORIANS OR POLITICIANS, but what we do has everything to do with history and politics—with industrialization, subsidies, and capitalism (or greed). The history of meat and meat workers—a group that includes butchers, farmers, laborers, and slaughterers—starts grim and brutal and just gets worse. Animals went from living outside and eating their natural diets to being lab-engineered to live stacked on top of one another by the thousands in order to (over)feed Americans now suffering from all kinds of diet-related health problems. Confining animals in large numbers and feeding them crap (literally) of course requires the use of antibiotics to keep them from getting sick. That's on top of the hormones they are administered to make them grow bigger, faster. Antibiotics overuse has led to superbugs—drug-resistant strains of bacteria— that threaten livestock as well as humans. And the confined animals' collective waste has become—no shocker here—an environmental disaster.

Then there's the slaughter. The volume of what goes through enormous processing plants and the speed at which it goes through are (partially) responsible for the massive recalls of E. coli–contaminated ground meat. It is common sense that this system of mass-producing animals isn't healthy for anyone. Since animal farms became industrialized, the treatment of animals has steadily worsened and labor issues have increased. Most people are familiar with some version of this scenario if they seek out a grass-fed and organic butcher who deals with whole local animals. It's certainly the reason many of our customers come to us and why we started our butcher shop: to be able to offer people a safer, viable alternative—especially since toxic chemicals accumulate in flesh, making meat one of the most contaminated choices in our food chain.

How all this went disgustingly, appallingly wrong is a horror story worth knowing. Others have brilliantly written the story of the industrialization of meat and all that that entails; we list our favorites on page 235. We urge you to read at least one of them. Here's our very truncated, butcher-centric version.

WHERE THINGS WENT WRONG

A few generations back, people ate free-roaming, free-foraging animals. These might even have been raised at home—pigs are living compost piles, very handy for kitchen and garden scraps. And chickens do triple duty: they eat ticks and other pests, produce eggs, and can eventually be stewed. Other animals can also be handy if you have a lot of space; ruminants, for example, cut the grass by eating it, then redistribute seeds and keep them fertilized with their manure. They also turn what humans don't eat (grass) into what we do (burgers, milk, cheese). It's a good, natural system. If you didn't keep animals, you got their products from someone who did. But the population grew, industrialization happened, and meat from animals

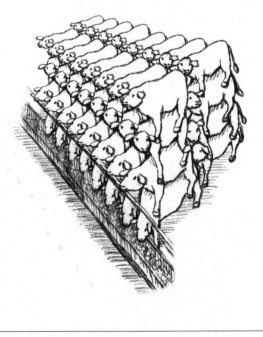

grown and slaughtered en masse in the middle of the country then transported around became—and remains—cheaper than meat grown down the road. On the surface, anyway. And with the convenience and accessibility also came a change in cultural expectations. Back in my grandfather's day, and certainly my great-grandfather's, steak was a special-occasion kind of meal. The common man ate mainly stews and roasts and a whole lot of cheap offal. Jessica grew up eating tongue, liver, sweetbreads, and brains because her mother did before her. Only in modern times do we expect to eat meat three times a day and consider a 20-ounce steak to be an individual portion.

Factory farming is a fairly recent phenomenon. The raising of animals moved from outdoors to indoors around the 1920s. Confinement operations began with chickens—the small guys are easiest to confine—and moved on to larger animals. Hog farming was soon similarly mechanized. Ruminants to this day still spend some portion of their lives on pasture, but then they are confined to feedlots to fatten up before slaughter. Of course that many animals crowded together get sick, and some die. So some brilliant schmuck came up with the idea of giving confinement animals preemptive doses of antibiotics. It keeps them from getting ill, but it also created those freaky superbugs, screwing us all and especially the workers. One Johns Hopkins study says poultry factory workers are thirty-two times more likely to be infected with drug-resistant E. coli than people who hold other jobs. For the record, we've never gotten sick in all the years we have owned the shop, and I've eaten everything in here raw. Antibiotics keep ruminants alive while they're being intensively fed corn along with protein supplements in feedlots; their multiple stomachs aren't designed to eat this mix and it makes them deathly ill when they do. The drugs and their effects are far-reaching—livestock antibiotics have been found in vegetables fertilized with manure.

To create more product faster, some other genius had the brilliant idea to hop animals up on synthetic growth hormones, the same kind of stuff that weight lifters use. For a while diethylstilbestrol (DES) was used, but that was banned in 1979 because it causes cancer. This was practically

Only in modern times do we expect to eat meat three times a day and consider a 20-ounce steak to be an individual portion.

WILD ANIMALS?

The unfathomable numbers of animals currently raised as food are not part of any natural ecosystem. Livestock aren't the same thing as wild animals. If we didn't want them for dinner, they wouldn't be here. And if we released them all into the wild in a mass vegan fantasy, they wouldn't survive. This is an important thing to understand. Also important: no matter how you raise them, livestock, like McMansions, aren't the most environmentally friendly things going. They require a lot of water, food, and land. They create greenhouse gases and contribute to global warming. But most Americans aren't going to stop eating meat entirely. And the argument can be made that tofu from pesticide-intensive, genetically modified soy crops isn't hugely eco, either. There are ways for carnivores to drastically lower the impact of what's on their plates. The first is to avoid conventional meat. The second is to eat locally and only whole, not processed, foods.

a decade *after* the drug was banned for use in pregnant women (it was thought to reduce the risk of complications but instead led to cancer plus reproductive issues in "DES daughters" and other, lesser health concerns for "DES sons"). Now other synthetic hormones are used. Hormone use in hogs and poultry is not permitted by the USDA, but it is allowed for cows/steers and sheep. Giving hormones to ruminants is outlawed in Europe, where it is deemed a health risk. American hormone-filled beef has been banned from being sold in Europe, Japan, and Canada at various times. There have been many politically charged repeals and rein-

statements of these bans to date. If it isn't immediately apparent to you why it is a bad idea to eat meat from an animal that has been given hormones, allow us to clarify: Those hormones remain in the meat postslaughter. You are eating them. Messing with your hormone levels can lead to all kinds of diseases, and if your system is developing—like kids' are—it's no joke. Livestock hormones have been linked to early puberty and cancer.

Animal feed developed in an equally terrifying fashion. This is a pennies business. You need to use every last scrap of the animal, and do it on a very large scale, to make any money. To do this, in the

conventional food system, postslaughter waste (blood, bone chips, meat slurry, and other things you don't want to think about) is repurposed into feed. Reprocessing agricultural waste—the ultimate bad idea—leads to persistent salmonella and the brain-wasting illness BSE (bovine spongiform encephalopathy), aka mad cow disease. The government backtracked some once it realized these enormous mistakes, adding regulations for mad cow after the fact. Cows and steers—natural vegetarians—are no longer permitted to eat themselves. But there are loopholes: they are still allowed to eat scraps from other animals, including animals that eat their scraps. No telling what bit of themselves steers might eat when munching on poultry manure. Yes, you read that right. Our government considers bird shit ac-

ceptable cattle feed. But the main thing all of these conventional animals are eating is corn. This government-subsidized corn is usually genetically modified, and it requires heavy use of petroleum-derived fertilizers and synthetic pesticides and irrigation to grow. So if you're eating conventional meat, you're eating all that stuff, too. The amount of oil and petroleum-based chemicals used to grow the corn to feed the vast hordes of conventionally raised animals in this country is staggering.

Not only do most Americans have access mainly to a falsely cheap, inhumane food supply that is making everyone *and* the planet sick, but factory farming also means we've lost sight of where our food comes from. Literally. You can't see animals that are confined inside. You can drive past factory farms containing hundreds of thousands of animals and never actually lay eyes on one (though you will smell their waste). It's another reason we feel whole animal butchery is so important: it brings us and our customers so much closer to dinner. We can look it in the eye. When you do this, you won't take for granted what's behind your dinner: a living, breathing animal and the farmer who raised it.

One more consequence of factory farming is the waste problem. Those confined animals create mountains of shit that has nowhere to go. There is no land under hoof to fertilize, only concrete. So they live in it. This creates unbearable air pollution—greenhouse gases and fumes that sicken the animals as well as the people unfortunate enough to live near factory farms. Waste is removed, mixed with water, and placed in "lagoons." (The Natural Resources Defense Council refers to these as "cesspools of shame.") They can leak. When they need to be emptied, this hazardous sludge, which contains hormone and antibiotic residue (it's estimated that 75 percent of the antibiotics animals ingest are excreted), sometimes E. coli, and other toxic chemicals, is then sprayed (particularly bad if the weather is windy or wet) or spread on the eroded land as fertilizer. From here, it enters our water in two ways: it seeps down into the groundwater, and, if it rains, it runs right off into our waterways. It's well documented that the chemicals in this mix contaminate our drinking and swimming water and lead to algae blooms that kill fish and aquatic life. Raw manure is up to 160 times more toxic than raw municipal sewage. It is literally a crappy system.

THE ORGANIC WAY

People have been farming organically forever, but since the government defined and standardized this method of farming and permitted people adhering to their regulations to use the USDA organic seal, it has fast become the number one alternative to conventional. Because farms must be third-party certified to use the logo, food carrying it—especially domestic, which is *far* more regulated than imported USDA organic (look for country of origin labels)—offers a level of trust. The regulations state that certified USDA organic animals must be raised "under conditions which provide for exercise and freedom of movement." Their feed is produced without the use of insecticides, pesticides, or genetic engineering, and it is free from sewage sludge and animal-derived proteins. No antibiotics or added hormones may be administered to the animals. Sick animals that require antibiotics must be removed from organic production. Meat is processed according to strictly defined standards, which restrict the use of chemicals and prohibit irradiation (zapping to kill bacteria). Animal waste must be dealt with according to safe composting standards. All good things. That said, it's not a perfect system. Most certified organic animals in this country are raised on large farms similar to conventional ones, minus hormones, antibiotics, and pesticides in the feed. Organic beef, for example, might be finished in big feedlots on organic corn and little or no grass. Animals are sometimes trucked very far between farm and feedlot, then again from feedlot to slaughterhouse—not very humane. It's rarely a local product. And not all of it is technically completely organic, because there are exemptions to the certification requirements. These include items that aren't easy to grow organically, like certain spices, or those difficult to source, like sausage casings. There are also degrees of how organic something actually is (see below).

THE PASTURED WAY

Our customers don't ask much about factory farms, but they're always asking about organic; in their minds the term *organic* negates factory farming. We actually prefer local and sustainable to certified organic. Everything in our cases is free-range: it grows on grass, in a situation you'd think of when you imagine a farm. Our farmers don't use hormones or antibiotics or pesticides or genetically modi-

READ ALL LABELS

Even the USDA organic label must be read carefully. Most people see the circle stamp or the word *organic* and go ahead and buy, not knowing there are actually shades of organic. Meat products like sausage or ham that are 100 percent organic are labeled "100 percent organic" (even though they may contain items on the organic exemption list, like nonorganic sausage casings). Those that are 95 percent organic may be labeled "organic." Products made using ingredients that are more than 70 percent organic may be labeled "made with organic ingredients." Think about what that other 30 percent might be when it comes to something like sausage.

fied feed. Certified organic feed would be ideal, but since it costs three times what regular feed costs and it isn't always local, we ask only that our farmers use sustainable, unsprayed feed. This tends to mean what they're growing on the same land the animals are roaming, usually corn.

We source the animals; we know the farmers; we know their backgrounds; we know if they're breeding or, if not, where they're getting their animals. We watch how many animals are on how many acres (crucial for them and for the land); we know our small slaughterhouse guys. And we don't deviate from the people we know and trust. We have a rhythm and we stick to it. That is traceability. We can't control everything, but this system allows us to see if and when anything starts to fall out of line. And we do not hesitate to drop

producers who do not appear to be or are unwilling to adhere to our standards.

Pasturing animals is a farming system that enhances soil fertility, conserves water, and produces fewer greenhouse gases. So does raising animals on farms close to where they will eventually be processed and eaten, instead of trucking them several times over the course of their lives. Some people argue that pastured animals create as much methane (livestock contribute as much as 20 percent globally of this nasty greenhouse gas) as conventionally raised ones do, via burping and farting; others claim the opposite. Even if pastured animals created the exact same amount of methane, they don't require fossil fuels and fertilizers, and their drug-filled waste isn't leaching directly into our waterways.

SLAUGHTER

Industrial farming has changed not only the way animals are raised but also the way they are killed. It's not that slaughter was ever kind, but industrialization brought a scale and efficiency to it that is straight out of a science fiction nightmare. We'd like to say one thing about slaughter—past, present, or future—up front: it is not humane. You can make the animals more comfortable as they move toward slaughter—and this is what is generally referred to as "humane"—but make no mistake: slaughter is slaughter. Animals are being killed to feed us. And someone has to do the killing—grim work that takes skill and patience. People e-mail us from around the country to ask questions about "humane slaughter." They want us to elaborate on the process because they like to be socially responsible. These are tough questions for us to answer. There are standards regarding the humane treatment of animals at slaughterhouses involving how they're shipped, loaded on and off trucks, handled, stunned, and killed. You try to be as kind and ethical as possible, but the fact is you are taking an animal's life that has been raised solely so you can eat it. You can't dress that up and put a bow on it. We've been at slaughters, and it's amazing how quickly something stops being an animal. When the life is gone, it's meat. So we try to explain to curious customers how it goes. Steers are stunned by a shot in the head—pigs and lambs are stunned with an electric rod—then they are hung up and their throats are cut so that they can bleed out as quickly and efficiently as possible. Chicken slaughter is typically done like this: The birds are hung upside down, still alive, and dragged through

COPING MECHANISM

There are many different ways to cope with the reality of slaughter. Some of our customers try humor; they e-mail us original limericks to read to the animals as their last rites, like:

Oh you, the cow from Kilamore,
A cow I vaguely do adore—
This poem's for you
To read as you moo,
A sound I'm afraid you'll make no more.

(Reprinted with permission)

electrified water to stun them. Then their throats are slit. Human beings are remarkably compartmentalized thinkers—especially when it comes to what they eat—so for many people this information is hard to take.

These days the process of slaughter in some large-scale mechanized facilities isn't actually that different from how it is done in small, local, family-owned ones or even bigger organic ones, thanks to the work of Temple Grandin, who is an animal behavior expert, a professor, and a bestselling author. Before she designed humane handling systems for half the cattle-processing facilities in the United States, animals weren't treated well at the slaughterhouse (to say the least) and some still are not. Grandin is autistic, and she has said this makes her think visually, like an animal. She sees what might be scaring animals or putting them off, including simple things like shadows, chains, and waving flags. Corporations like McDonald's have hired her to consult; as it turns out, a humane slaughterhouse is a much more efficient one. We're clearly not fans of the Golden Arches, nor are we advocating killing thousands of animals in an hour, but her basic scoring system, which answers important questions—Are the animals making noise (happy animals are quiet animals)? Are they stressed? Are they cold or wet? Have they been fed or

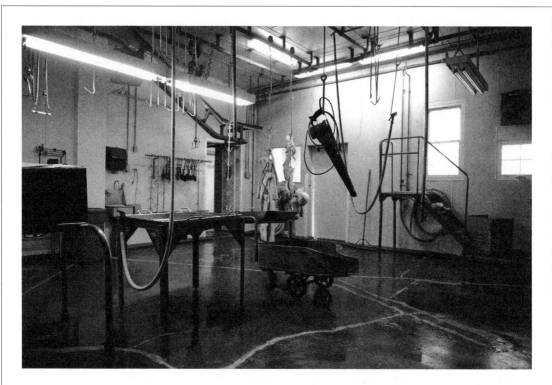

watered?—has dramatically changed the process for the better, decreasing fear and pain for untold numbers of animals in their final hours. Even People for the Ethical Treatment of Animals (PETA) likes her—they gave her an award in 2004. Grandin's work is so far-reaching that HBO made an Emmy award–winning film about it in 2009. Still, some enormous meat-processing operations don't follow her guidelines. And even in the ones that do—as well as in small, local slaughterhouses—the time spent slaughtering and the skills vary wildly. No two slaughterhouses, big or small, are created equal.

We deal strictly with small, local slaughterhouses that kill from ten to fifteen steers per week and similarly low numbers of other animals; larger commercial processing plants slaughter as many as twenty-five thousand steers per day. We don't work with these vertically integrated factory-farm monster operations. Our animals are brought to our slaughterhouses from local farms with very little time in transit; travel stresses them. They are allowed to rest before being slaughtered. Unlike in an industrial setting, they are brought in one by one by a person.

The local slaughterhouse is a farmer's best friend. Despite the mass shift to factory farming, there are actually a fair number of farmers across the country raising good, pure, pastured animals. And there are plenty of shoppers who want that meat—more and more each day. But to get the good product to conscious consumers, farmers and butchers need small, local slaughterhouses. Without them, all animals would be processed in a huge plant. Medium-size plants that handle a thousand animals a day will sometimes serve small farmers, and theoretically there is traceability to make sure there are no mix-ups: you're supposed to get back the same animals you sent in. But we've heard some horror stories about farmers trying to sort their goods from the conventional. This all points to the fact that there aren't enough of the "artisanal abattoirs," as the *New York Times* calls them. And it's a big problem.

We have been quoted in article after article about this missing link. The media is finally paying attention to the fate of the small slaughterhouse, which is great though shocking, because it's not the sexiest of topics. The articles detail how many plants have closed in recent years due to costs, tight regulations, and politics (the powerful conglomerates want to and do dominate the market—as of this writing, *four* companies own the processing plants that are said to slaughter as much as 80 percent if not more of the animals killed in this country: Cargill, Tyson, JBS USA, and Smithfield). And they keep conglomerating. The statistics are bleak. We live and work in an area that has a fair number of small, local facilities, comparatively speaking. But apparently two decades ago New York State had twice the number of federally inspected slaughterhouses. You need to be federal to sell to butcher shops or across state lines. Across the country, hundreds of small slaughterhouses have closed during the past decade. And just because there are slaughterhouses and farms in any given state doesn't mean that the two shall easily meet. It's all about location, transportation, and booking slots—again, we are talking about family-owned businesses that process only ten to fifteen steers a week. If a farmer hasn't booked ahead or otherwise can't get a slot to have an animal processed when it reaches the optimum weight for slaughter, it will have to be sold at auction. A drug-free, pasture-raised animal doesn't necessarily fetch extra cash at a conventional auction, unfortunately.

Thankfully we're very well set up with our slaughterhouses—our slots are booked a year in advance. But this issue has

The local slaughterhouse is a farmer's best friend.

affected us in the past. When our original guy, Ted Johnson, retired, we had to hustle to find a new situation. And one time a fire burned a place we were working with to the ground. We had three animals hanging there. Luckily they were covered by our insurance, but we had nothing to sell that week or the next, and we lost all the slots we had lined up for the future. Still, we were far better off than the farmers—can you imagine raising an animal for two years only to have it just burn up?

Initiatives to build more local slaughterhouses as well as alternatives are starting to appear. Glynwood, a nonprofit organization near us, is working on a Northeast mobile slaughterhouse. It's a USDA-licensed large-animal meat-processing unit called a Modular Harvest System that travels to farms. For us, the best, safest, and cleanest solution would be to build more slaughterhouses, but that's expensive and controversial. We all want clean food, but it's the rare citizen who wants to live next to or near a slaughterhouse. And even if the money, the permits, and the location align, not too many people have the desire or the skills to do this difficult, low-paying work. For our slaughterhouse guys, it's a family business. They really know what they're doing. We respect them and rely on them. They're our ears and eyes; they see it all before we do—the guts, the flesh, the goods.

LABOR ISSUES

All of this talk about humane treatment begs another question: what about *human* treatment? We care about both. Although our customers ask us about the animals all the time, they almost *never* ask us about the workers who process them. We like to say that PETA should start a new branch—PETP: People for the Ethical Treatment of People. Processing animals isn't a glamorous job; it tends to be done by immigrants, many of whom are here illegally and therefore unable to join a union. The work is dangerous; the conventional disassembly lines are fast and furious. Most workers have no health insurance or workers' comp to rely on when they get hurt, which happens often. By all accounts many live in slave-like conditions—in overstuffed shacks near the packinghouses. Industrial slaughterhouse workers are said to suffer from high levels of depression and substance abuse.

The farms and slaughterhouses we work with rarely employ workers who aren't family. If they need extra help, they tend to hire locals. Laborers are part of this system and deserve consideration. They're the invisible link that gets food to your table.

A BRIEF HISTORY OF BUTCHER SHOPS

Historically whole animals went to butcher shops after slaughter. How butchers and their shops evolved in New York provides a window into the development of the profession across America. Our friend Suzanne Wasserman, the historian and filmmaker, knows everything there is to know about New York City's history, including its butchers. According to Suzanne, from colonial times to about 1840, being a butcher was a revered, insular, aristocratic, even political career. Butchers back then were from England and members of an exclusive guild. They passed their skills down from father to son. Apprenticeship took years (and truthfully it still does). There were no actual butcher shops; meat was only allowed to be sold in public markets. But in the 1840s, during a period of mass immigration, skilled German and Irish butchers arrived. They were excluded from the guild, so they set up illegal butcher shops. Eventually the city council realized it couldn't stop the shops, so in 1843 it gave guild status to all of these butchers and legalized the sale of meat in private shops. By 1850, there were 531 shops, and half of the city's butchers were foreign born.

The animals these butchers carved came mainly from farms in Westchester and New Jersey (the Garden State earned

its name legitimately). They were herded through the streets of New York to public and private slaughterhouses located largely along the rivers. Apprentices would pick up the carcasses at the slaughterhouses and bring them back to the shops on meat carts that were considered a big public nuisance and became the topic of much debate. We don't doubt it— we get flack from people who don't like to see our carts, loaded high with whole animals, wheeled from the street to the back of the shop, so we can only imagine what it was like back in the day with carcasses rolling all over the city.

Modernization and economics changed everything. By the mid-nineteenth century, according to Suzanne, meat production began to shift to the Midwest because of economies of scale. With the development of refrigerated train cars, meat could be transported far and wide, and things began to change for the worse. Modernization was also at the heart of the near-death of the small butcher shop. The one-two punch was the rise of home refrigeration, which eliminated the need to shop for meat daily, and the convenient one-stop shopping of supermarkets that took off after World War II. The situation continued to decline, and before long the ease of precut boxed meat sold in those supermarkets impinged on real butcher shops. Butchers were no longer required to butcher. Shops unable to compete with

grocery stores providing larger quantities of the same cuts went out of business. Gentrification also pushed many butcher shops out of neighborhoods where they had been mainstays. We now have a generation of people who live on prepared foods, frozen dinners, and takeout, and who don't know how to cook.

Today, butcher shops in New York and across the country are rare, but a revival is going on that is being driven by the sustainable meat movement. Reviving butcher shops isn't easy because butchering is an art, one that has been nearly lost. Butchers didn't want their educated grandsons to take up the family business. They wanted them to be doctors and lawyers. Working with your hands, once considered skilled labor, wasn't thought of as an honorable profession for a while. But the current generation seems to feel differently. We get Ivy League grads wanting to enroll in our apprentice program at Fleisher's. They don't want to sit at a desk in front of a computer all day. They want to do something useful and work with sustainable meat. It's not blue-collar anymore, it's green-collar.

It even took a while for our parents to understand why we would want to do what we do, but once we made it into the *New York Times* they seemed to stop worrying. After all, what New York Jew wouldn't want his or her kid featured in the *Times*? We are working to reclaim and then teach the craft that has been abandoned. You can't learn it in culinary school—that curriculum is all about cutting or portioning precut boxed parts. Butchering whole animals has always been a skill passed down, and we are returning to that tradition.

THE ART OF
BUTCHERY

PEERING OVER OUR CASES, customers can see the table where we spend most of our day cutting meat. We break or cut on a large communal wooden table—a former baking table we bought years ago. When you bench-break—break down or cut carcasses on a table—you don't need high ceilings, hooks, or gadgets; a solid table and sharp knives will do. Bench breaking is not the industry standard, but we find hook breaking—cutting carcasses on a hook hung from the ceiling—too dangerous. Hook breaking is useful when handling a lot of beef all the time, as in a slaughterhouse or a packinghouse; using rails hung with hooks makes it easier to move huge carcasses. Industrial meat workers wear hard hats for a reason: if a hook falls on you, it will kill you. At the shop, some pieces of beef weigh upwards of 200 pounds. It sounds absurd when I say that I have had an arm chuck fall on me, but the hook it was hanging on almost severed my carotid artery as I lifted it off a rack. One of my employees was once pinned by a pig pile in the cooler. It sounds funny until you realize no one could hear him screaming for help—our walk-ins are that big and that insulated.

In our shop, we bench-break right out front for many reasons. The main one is that we want our customers to see where their food comes from. The farmer and activist Joel Salatin believes that what America needs is glass abattoirs, and we agree. If consumers truly knew what went on behind the cement-block walls of most slaughterhouses they would never eat conventional meat again. We believe, as Salatin does, in transparency. Let people see the process—the line between animal and meat—and do it with grace and understanding. Though the slaughterhouse reality is not available to customers, we want to, and are able to, bring them closer to their food. We want all our customers to be fully aware of what we do and why we do it. By allowing them to watch, we are making them complicit. Some people shy away from the reality, but most are fascinated by what we do. They hang over the counter to watch us cut primals into parts, band-saw our way through mountains of bones, and tenderize their steaks. If we're out of something in our cases, we'll go into the cooler, grab a primal, lug it to the table, and carve it out for you. That's what we mean by being a custom-cut shop. It might take a few minutes, but you can watch as you wait. Almost every new customer remarks on how it reminds them of the butcher shops of their youth.

The real craft of the butcher is not just the cutting—that's necessary, of

course, and the swashbuckling aspect of it sure makes it fun—but knowing how to read a carcass. As we cut, we are reading the flesh, checking and double-checking it. Our first set of eyes is at the slaughterhouse—our guys will always call us if there's a problem, though there rarely is. They're on the lookout for things like stomach content and the health of the animal, and are backed up by a USDA inspector and a vet who check every animal both before and after it has been killed. The only time I have ever sent back an animal was because the slaughterhouse called me with serious concerns about the treatment of a veal calf brought in for us.

Our guys could tell the animal had been dehydrated by the way the hide peeled away from the carcass and how the muscle felt. I was advised not to take the carcass, but I didn't have to be told never to deal with that farmer again. Outside of something rare like that, the only other reason we would send something back is if it were a *dark cutter:* this is the term for a carcass with dark flesh, which is usually the sign of a poorly raised animal subjected to a combination of stressful factors during its lifetime—perhaps it wasn't well handled, or maybe it was traumatized. A dark cutter's meat is almost inedible—sour, bitter, metallic, and tough. We can't do anything with it, not even grind it for dog food. (Of course, most processors would run it through grinders and it ends up in your burgers.)

When the animals come into the shop, we run through a mental checklist. First, we look for the ubiquitous blue USDA stamp. Though we trust our slaughterhouses, by law we can't sell retail—and our wholesale customers can't serve meat in their restaurants—without this seal. Next, we check the carcasses' weight to evaluate shrinkage and to estimate our yields. Animals are bought at "live" weight or "hot" hanging weight. We buy ours usually at "hot" weight and receive them as "cold" weight. Live is literally on the hoof; hot is the unchilled weight of a beef carcass after the hide, head, gastrointestinal tract, and internal organs have been removed;

Sometimes I feel like a medical examiner trying to figure out how various injuries might have occurred.

cold is what it sounds like—chilled. With lambs, the heads are not removed. Lambs are skinned, but pigs are never stripped of their hides; too much fat is lost when peeling hogs. Fat is flavor. It's also money. So we won't work with a slaughterhouse that peels pigs. Our pigs are scalded, and we expect to get clean, hairless hides. All these weights break down into something called a *dressing percentage,* a term hunters may be familiar with. We figure we lose up to 4 percent between hot and cold weight in the first twenty-four hours—on muscle shrinkage or evaporation alone. The loss doesn't sound like much, but it currently translates into $30,000 to $40,000 a year. We have bought our animals in other ways in the past (estimated live weight, for example, turned out to be a complete rip-off for us; after all, it's hard to guesstimate the size of the animal on the hoof). We would love to buy cold, but our farmers don't sell that way—they would lose money, absorbing the shrinkage loss themselves. We factor our current deal into our percentages, markups, and yields.

Yield is crucial, so the next thing we calculate is the fat-to-meat ratio. If an animal comes in too small, we lose money; if

it comes in too large, we also lose money. There's not enough meat if the animal is too skinny; we are paying for fat if the animal is too large. Then we carefully examine the outside of the carcasses for bruising and other telltale signs of overcrowding, to make sure that what our farmers are telling us about how they raise their animals is true. Bruises look like bruises on humans—a dark patch or contusion—underneath which you often see injury to the muscle. When we find bruises, we have to cut out the whole area and toss it. Sometimes I feel like a medical examiner trying to figure out how various injuries might have occurred. I have no real way of knowing, but I believe this kind of bruising doesn't happen in shipping; it wouldn't show up that fast.

We root through the boxes of offal as soon as we get them. Hearts, livers, and tongues are removed immediately and sent to us the same week the animal is killed. The carcasses remain at the slaughterhouse for another week, chilling and aging. We examine the offal for clues; it tells us so much. We look for livers the color of oxblood that are rich, smooth, and heavy with blood, indicating both

a fresh kill and a healthy animal. We like to see hearts that are firm and lean, with a heavy fat cap surrounding them—nothing viscous or sticky—proving that these are normal, strong muscles that pumped the blood free and clear of the organ.

We also check the eyes of the pigs (whose severed heads come in boxes) and lambs (whose heads arrive attached to the carcass). The eyes should be clear, not slimy, and never sunken—like what my grandmother used to say about those of a good fish. We don't get steer heads: our steers are shot in the head to stun them before slaughter, and our slaughter-houses, like most small plants, don't have the proper USDA-required head-washing cabinet to remove the resulting bone shards, so we can't sell any part of them

except the tongues. The heads are removed and discarded at the slaughter-house. This area has become more and more regulated of late. It's a shame because beef cheeks are a delicacy. Our pigs are not shot in the head, so we console ourselves with pork cheeks—truly one of my favorite snacks.

As we begin to cut up the carcass, we look for signs of internal bruising and broken bones. These injuries sometimes happen during transport or slaughter, even with well-handled animals; after all, they are crammed in the back of a truck and aren't wearing seatbelts! By looking at the way the blood blooms around the wound, it's easy for us to tell if it happened postslaughter. If injuries happen too often, that spells trouble. On pigs, we look at the incision made when the pig is exsanguinated with a knife sometimes referred to as a pig sticker. It doesn't affect the already-dead pig, but if the cut is too deep, we lose up to a pound of product. Butchery is a numbers game, and we need to make every bit of our animals count.

As we continue to break down the animal, we look for several other signs. Moist, firm muscle is as imperative as strong bones that cut easily and don't shatter. With pigs, we pay attention to how the skins pull off the fat and flesh. With beef and lamb, the way the fat covers the muscle and interweaves throughout it (aka marbling) is something we check every step of the way. Processors pay a meat grader to grade their carcasses as prime, choice, or select—USDA designations based on this fat content. Most meats sold in supermarkets are graded at choice or select; prime is the fattiest of the lot and is usually only found at top-end restaurants. Pastured animals aren't graded because they have less intramuscular fat. If you think you're missing out on something by buying grass-fed meat instead of the conventionally raised stuff, just keep in mind that there's a lot more to great-tasting meat than the grade. It's apples and oranges.

We also look for scar tissue as we work our way through the carcass, especially in the bottom rounds; this is where we would expect to find injection sites that our animals shouldn't have. To date we haven't found any. We are also especially careful when looking at a veal's bottom round for blemishes like bedsores that come from leaning excessively against a stall.

Occasionally we find tumors or abscesses. They come in all shapes and sizes and are uniformly gross. Often these tumors mean nothing—their source could be bruising or even an ingrown hair. Sometimes, though, they are a sign of overbreeding and overcrowding. Once we had to stop dealing with a pig farmer whose hogs started coming in regularly with tumors. Though it may seem otherwise, the odd abscess can actually be a good thing; it is proof positive that the animals are not receiving prophylactic antibiotics.

PRIMAL PRIMER

Beef, lamb, and pork all have four legs, so technically they can all be broken down into the same primals, which is what slaughterhouses and butchers call the large basic cuts initially carved from the carcass. From there they could also be cut into the same subprimals and cuts. But that's not how it's done. Primal names are different from animal to animal. And you don't really want to pull muscles out of the primals of different animals and use them all the same way. A beef flank is one thing, but a pork flank belongs on a belly, cured and smoked. That's bacon.

Carcasses can be cut in many different ways, depending on seasonality, location, and demand. What sells in the winter—roasts and braising cuts—are turned into steaks or grind in the summer. The rest of the world does not butcher the same way Americans do. You can really get to know how cultures live and eat based on how they cut their meat. The Spanish leave the sirloin on their hams (this is known as an *ibérico* cut) because they know that their *jamón* is in greater demand than a sirloin roast. Smart folks—doing this increases the amount of muscle they have to work with. An employee of ours learned her trade in Mexico, and one day for fun we had her cut as if she were still there. We learned that there are an awful lot of ways to make meat for tacos out of a side of beef. Demand guides our work. Our style of cutting depends on what our customers want to eat; it has to sell, or else we would be out of business.

What most people don't realize when they're standing in front of our cases—and it's something that you can't notice when looking at a multitude of industrial meat—is that the cuts you get from a carcass depend on the cuts you get from a carcass. Let me explain. If you cut a porterhouse steak from the short loin—this is the subprimal that contains the New York strip and the filet, with no sirloin attached—you can't also have a boneless strip, a bone-in strip, or a filet mignon. Where and how you cut limits the other cuts available. Do you want country-style ribs? Then there's no boneless shoulder roast for you. We are always weighing the options with customer demand to make the most beneficial choices.

It's the rare customer who actually knows where on the animal that strip or those country-style ribs came from. But this knowledge is important: it helps you understand how to cook your meat. Muscles that get worked hard in an animal's life will be tougher, and need to be stewed, braised, or slowly smoked until tender, while underutilized muscles, like tenderloin, barely need to be cooked at all. Jessica likes to use the human body to show customers the breakdown of where cuts come from. Your butt constitutes a beef top round, your pecs a brisket. As odd as it seems, this comparison works to help people understand the meat. After all, muscle is muscle. People do really get where this chop or that shank comes from once they think about it in terms of the structure and musculature of their own bodies. It also helps to explain "worked" versus "unworked" muscle. The neck on every animal will be worked extensively since it is moving constantly and holding the head up. And you know from your own experience that the muscles in our legs (even if we only have two) are getting the most exercise and are therefore tougher than our bellies, which are often more like a foie gras duck's liver—fatty and bloated. The real difference between farm animal and human musculature is those two legs. Because humans walk upright, our filet mignon would suck; those are the muscles we use to support our stance. If you're on all fours, your back is a broad and somewhat immobile, relatively unworked structure that therefore houses the prime cuts like rib eyes, loin chops, and of course that ubiquitous tenderloin.

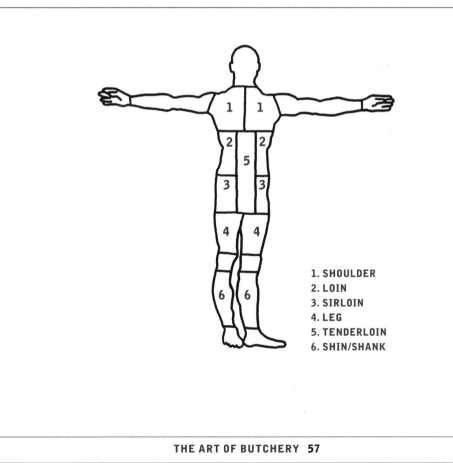

1. SHOULDER
2. LOIN
3. SIRLOIN
4. LEG
5. TENDERLOIN
6. SHIN/SHANK

CUTS TO MAKE YOUR BUTCHER CRAZY

Because we get whole animals, we are in the enviable position of having every available cut possible (with the exception of a few types of offal). This makes us the darlings of cookbook fanatics, Europeans, and trophy hunters. But we always wonder what folks do when a recipe calls for flanken-style short ribs or sirloin top shaved paper-thin for shabu-shabu and they don't have a butcher who is up to the challenge. If you want to see your butcher sweat, ask him or her for one of these cuts:

SHABU-SHABU This Japanese dish is based on whisper-thin slices of beef that get dragged through hot stock to barely cook them. Your butcher needs to partially freeze a sirloin top and shave slices off it with a deli slicer. We do this all the time (it's one of our favorite winter meals), but it's special order only.

FLANKEN Taken from the steer's rib plate, flanken is really the same as short ribs but cut in a different way. Instead of cutting between and separating the ribs into the more commonplace 2 x 2-inch blocks or chunks, flanken short ribs are cut across the whole rib section, making a long, thin band of ribs joined together by strips of meat. Flanken is usually cut 1 inch thick and two to three ribs across. These short ribs are both thin and flavorful—great for grilling (see page 188).

TERES MAJOR This is the second most tender muscle in the animal's body so we have nicknamed it the faux filet. It comes from the top of the shoulder clod. Most butchers grind it (if they have ever even seen it).

SKIN-ON BONELESS CHICKEN BREASTS We believe that the only reason boneless skinless chicken breasts exist is because consumers demand the leanest cuts around. Okay, we get that, but to us the skin is a necessary addition that provides protection and flavor to an otherwise lackluster cut. We like stuffing our skin-on boneless breasts (think herb butter à la chicken Kiev). Sadly this doesn't seem to be an item high on anyone's list but ours.

TRI-TIP This triangularly shaped, deeply flavorful cut comes from the sirloin. There are two per steer and each weighs about 1.5 pounds (meaning there are 3 pounds per 800-pound animal). Tri-tip is the stuff of legendary barbecue in Santa Maria, California (near Santa Monica), and perhaps the reason for its full-on popularity on the West Coast (it's still relatively unknown back East). One of the oldest butcher shops in New York City, the Florence Meat Market, "invented" a steak based on this cut—the Newport steak, named after the crescent moon that appeared on the Newport cigarette package. If you are not in California or New York, it might be impossible to find.

PRIMAL BASICS

There are many different methods and ways of breaking down a whole animal into parts. The industry standard is to break down all animals into four basic primals per side—eight total. Outside conventional butchery, everyone has his or her own particular way. We do it a little differently at Fleisher's, which we explain in detail throughout these pages.

These are the standard versions:

LAMB/VEAL	PORK	BEEF
Shoulder (Chuck)	Belly	Chuck
Rack (Rib)	Shoulder (Butt/Picnic)	Rib
Loin	Loin	Loin
Leg	Ham	Round

OFFAL

Offal is exactly what's implied by the term *nose-to-tail eating,* and it's part of any sustainable butcher shop. In recent years, offal—the internal organs and entrails of an animal as well as some external parts like tails, testicles, and ears—has become increasingly trendy. There are chefs who have built their entire reputations on serving things that some folks think should be dumped in the trash. (People tend to order it at restaurants more than they make it at home.) The funny thing is, this is how people have always eaten, and most of us have unwittingly dined on offal or make certain exceptions when it pleases us. We have lots of customers who turn their noses up at kidneys or fries (that's balls to you), but who scarf down foie gras the first chance they get. Almost everyone who has come into our shop tries our sausages, but no one has ever remarked that they are grossed out by the fact that we use natural casings (lamb and pig intestines). But throw a whole beef tongue on the table and watch people get woozy. It doesn't help that offal is pronounced a lot like "awful." Some parts, like brains and fries, are so bland that we can't figure out what people are getting so excited about (*I know, I know, it's a texture thing*), but a nice pâté, an oxtail stew, a blood sausage—now that's something to get worked up about.

Americans seem to have forgotten that

their ancestors, many of whom could afford little else in terms of meat, ate a lot of offal—it was cheap, nutritious, and in those days easily accessible. In most parts of Europe and Asia folks still eat this way, and it's an accepted fact that no part of the animal should go to waste. You can (and should) eat every part of the pig except the squeal. The cookbooks that we love the most and find most inspirational— including *The River Cottage Meat Book,* by Hugh Fearnley-Whittingstall; *The Whole Beast: Nose to Tail Eating,* by Fergus Henderson; and *Pork and Sons,* by Stéphane Reynaud—echo this sentiment. Offal is not only good food; eating it demonstrates a certain respect for the animal.

So, tap into your heritage (or try someone else's on for size) and get yourself a taste of chopped liver with schmaltz and gribbnitz (chicken fat and skin), haggis, steak and kidney pie, liverwurst, chitterlings (pig intestines), scrapple, southern fried giblets, curried oxtail, and tendon soup.

That said, it isn't always easy to find these "variety meats," as supermarkets today seem to specialize in grinds and primes. Even most butcher shops get boxed meat, which precludes their ability to provide their customers with anything racier than chicken livers. If you want offal, your best bet is to make friends with a good butcher or a farmer and order in advance. Even we don't keep our offal in

our cases—it's special order only. And as much as we would like to provide everything, we can't. As we've said, due to slaughterhouse regulations we don't get beef/veal brains, beef cheeks, or tripe. If you are desperate to sample uterus, chicken feet, or spleen, try ethnic markets or your local Chinatown but know that it's highly unlikely these will be from local sustainably raised and pastured animals.

When you buy offal, keep in mind that it needs to be very fresh, especially kidneys, which quickly turn, taste bitter, and smell of urine (of course). A kidney should look glistening and be firm to the touch. If the offal is dry, cracked, or smells off, don't buy it and sure as hell don't eat it. Liver and oxtails are probably the most widely available offal and are as simple to cook as a steak or a beef stew, but far less expensive. Offal should be consumed immediately upon cooking, though pâtés and terrines can be stored for a week or so. Most offal can be frozen. That's how we sell most of our beef liver. Eating nose to tail may be a crucial part of being an ethical carnivore, but people just don't ask for it. Whatever doesn't sell goes into our raw dog food (along with chicken, chicken bones, tongue, hearts, and kidneys). Some lucky dogs are eating their way through 200 to 300 pounds of it per week—at least someone is appreciating our offal offerings.

THE DOG'S DINNER

People always think we must have the luckiest dogs in the world. Sure, they get occasional leftover steak and they certainly have buried so many bones in our backyard that we are just waiting for CSI to pay us a visit. But what they, and many of our customers' dogs as well as cats, live on is Fleisher's raw pet food. It's made of chicken and chicken bones plus beef heart, liver, and tongues, all ground together. It's great for them and us—pet food is a sustainable use of beef offal. We freeze it into patties and sell a cooler's worth of it weekly. We also have liver treats we sell out of every week. Our furry friends love it.

TREATS

We have two dogs that we love dearly and who eat better than a lot of people we know. Our customers seem to care for (and feed) their dogs in the same manner that we do—well and with love. We created this treat especially for our customers' pets, whose names we often know even if we don't know their owners'.

It will keep your neighbor's dog from howling at midnight for at least a week . . .

❖ Preheat the oven to 350°F.

❖ Dice 1 beef liver into 1- to 1½-inch pieces.

❖ Put the liver chunks in a roasting pan and roast for 30 minutes, until they are firm and slightly dry to the touch.

❖ Cool and store in an airtight container. They can be left out for a day or two; after that, refrigerate.

OFFALLY GOOD

KIDNEY

Lamb kidneys encased in fat are about ¼ pound each; figure one per person. Pig and veal kidneys are larger; one feeds two people. One beef kidney feeds three. Most requests for kidneys come from our British customers and we love them for it. This is the cooking method we always suggest: throw the kidneys in a pot and boil the piss out of 'em. (We never miss a chance to use old butcher humor.) But boiling is not actually the best way to prepare a kidney. Here's a better way:

❖ Try to purchase kidneys that are still covered in a shell of hard, white fat. This fat acts as a natural protector; when rendered, it is known as tallow in lamb or beef. In pigs, it's leaf lard.

❖ With a 5-inch knife, slit the fat that encapsulates each kidney, pry the slit open with your fingers, and gently pull the fat away from the kidney until it is all removed except for one small section at the underside of the lobe. Sever this section with the knife. Either render or discard the fat.

❖ Remove the thin, shiny membrane that surrounds each kidney by making an ⅛-inch slit in it with the knife. Ease it off carefully.

❖ Soak the prepared kidneys in milk overnight in the refrigerator. Rinse the kidneys after soaking and discard the milk.

❖ Cut each kidney in half, remove the core fat (the substance that attaches the kidney to the muscle), and slice the kidney into ½-inch pieces.

❖ Kidneys are best sautéed but release acrid juices into the pan (we weren't kidding about the piss), so they must be drained after they are browned. Season the kidneys with salt and pepper and quickly sauté them over medium-high heat in 1 tablespoon of olive oil or a combination of oil and butter for 4 to 5 minutes, or until they lose their pinkness.

❖ Drain the kidneys in a strainer set over a bowl and let rest for 5 minutes. Discard the pan juices. Wipe out the pan, heat again, and melt 2 tablespoons of butter. Add 2 tablespoons shallots or onions and cook until soft. Add a splash of white wine or a dash of stock (both couldn't hurt) and simmer until thickened, about 1½ minutes. Return the drained kidneys to the pan and warm through.

❖ Serve on buttered toast points.

HEART

Heart is an incredibly fussy thing to prepare. It needs to be cleaned well. Heart is a lean (the leanest cut of muscle in an animal's body) but fairly bland organ that lends itself well to searing or tartare, though the most commonly used cooking method seems to be braising. All of the fat found on the heart surrounds the actual muscle and must be removed.

❖ First, portion a beef or veal heart weighing 3 to 5 pounds into the naturally thinner and thicker sections. This sounds confusing, but it will make sense when you are standing in front of a heart; it is done so that you can control the timing when you cook the muscle.

❖ Remove the fat and skin until what is lying before you looks like it has been peeled like a grape. Remember to remove any gristle or valves from the interior of the heart as well.

❖ At this point you can cut the thin and thick sections into slices, toss them with some olive oil, salt, and pepper, and throw them into a very hot pan. We would suggest sautéing the slices for 2 to 3 minutes per side, depending on the thickness. Since the muscle is so lean, we like to cook it until rare to medium-rare.

❖ We plate heart with something rich and buttery; or give it a dash of good oil, which is the way we like to serve tenderloin.

There are chefs who have built their entire reputations on serving things that some folks think should be dumped in the trash.

The Best Ways to Cook Offal

So you buy some pig ears and take them home. Now what? Here are some tips on the best ways to cook ears, plus everything from brains to heart.

	Brains	Cheeks	Intestines/ Chitterlings	Ears	Feet	Fries	Gizzards
BEEF/VEAL							
Sauté	❖					❖	
Deep-fry	❖	❖				❖	
Grill							
Smoke		❖					
Roast							
Poach	❖					❖	
Braise		❖				❖	
LAMB							
Sauté	❖					❖	
Deep-fry	❖					❖	
Grill							
Smoke							
Roast							
Poach	❖					❖	
Braise						❖	
PIG							
Sauté	❖		❖	❖		❖	
Deep-fry	❖	❖	❖	❖	❖	❖	
Grill							
Smoke		❖		❖	❖		
Roast					❖		
Poach	❖		❖	❖	❖	❖	
Braise		❖	❖	❖	❖	❖	
POULTRY							
Sauté					❖		❖
Deep-fry					❖	❖	❖
Grill					❖		❖
Smoke					❖		
Roast					❖		
Poach					❖		
Braise						❖	❖

Heart	Kidney	Liver	Spleen	Stomach	Sweetbreads	Tails	Tongue	Tripe
✤	✤	✤			✤		✤	✤
		✤			✤		✤	
✤		✤			✤		✤	
✤		✤			✤	✤	✤	
✤		✤	✤		✤	✤	✤	
✤	✤				✤		✤	✤
✤	✤	✤	✤		✤	✤	✤	✤
✤	✤	✤			✤		✤	✤
		✤			✤		✤	
✤		✤			✤		✤	
✤					✤		✤	
✤		✤	✤		✤		✤	
✤	✤	✤			✤		✤	✤
✤	✤	✤	✤		✤		✤	✤
✤	✤	✤		✤				
		✤				✤	✤	
✤		✤					✤	
✤				✤		✤	✤	
✤		✤	✤	✤		✤	✤	
✤	✤	✤		✤		✤	✤	
✤	✤	✤	✤	✤		✤	✤	
✤		✤						
✤		✤						
✤		✤						
✤		✤						
		✤						
✤								

GREASE IS THE WORD

Part of nose-to-tail butchering is coming up with uses for fat, which makes up roughly 15 percent of an animal's body weight. Over the years we have gotten pretty creative—we have made beef tallow citronella candles (short-lived—they smelled like a barbecue gone horribly wrong) as well as lovely smelling tallow-based soaps. But mostly we just make our fat into chunks of tallow, blocks of lard, and tubs of duck fat for our customers to (hopefully) cook with.

Here's the skinny on what's what in the world of fats:

CAUL FAT is the fatty lining of a pig's stomach, which looks like a sheet of diaphanous webbing. It is used to wrap lean meats while roasting; this technique is called barding, and it imparts moisture into the meat as the fat melts.

DUCK FAT Is there anything better than duck fat? Use it to panfry potatoes, like they do in French bistros, or confit a couple of duck legs. Duck (and goose, too) fat is great, but often hard to come by.

FATBACK is the strip of fresh fat running down the pig's back. It is often cured to make the melt-in-your-mouth delicacy lardo, or it can just be rendered into lard.

LARD, or rendered pork fat, is nearly 100 percent fat, as opposed to butter, which is about 80 percent fat and 20 percent water. Though animal fats have gotten a bad reputation as heart-stoppers and artery-cloggers, lard is still well loved among bakers and intrepid cooks who prize its ability to produce flaky crusts and silky sauces. Lard has a high smoke point, making it exceptional for frying things like chicken (see page 212). It's also healthier than manufactured hydrogenated fats like most vegetable shortenings.

LEAF LARD is the dry, hard, crumbly fat cap that surrounds the kidney of the pig. This fat contains the fewest impurities, making it the gold standard for baking. Mix this with butter (a 1:1 butter-to-fat ratio is good) for the best piecrusts you have ever made.

SALT PORK is salted fat, usually cut from the belly or side of the pig. It is a great flavoring agent, especially for beans and greens. Use a chunk of it instead of the fat you'd normally use—just remember to season your dish judiciously.

SUET is raw (unprocessed or nonrendered) beef or lamb fat. What's sold in many supermarkets as suet is rarely unadulterated. That's actually tallow. We make suet cakes in the winter for our birds, but render the fat. It's easier to work with and shelf stable longer.

HOW TO RENDER FAT

It's simple to make high-quality lard or tallow that can be used for baking, cooking, or soap making. Fats should be stored in the refrigerator, where they will last for three months or can be frozen for a year. We like to cut our lard into manageable ½-pound chunks and freeze it—it defrosts quickly, and does not have to be defrosted in the refrigerator.

❖ Buy pork fat, beef suet, or lamb fat from your butcher shop or farmer. Make sure the fat is fresh, clean smelling, and not slimy. Whatever you render, count on getting a 75 percent return.

❖ Cut the fat into 1-inch squares and then finely dice it (we run ours through the meat grinder).

❖ Place the diced fat into a heavy-bottomed pan set over low heat. Melt the fat, without stirring, until it is literally a pool of oil. Alternatively, you can melt the fat in a Crock-Pot.

❖ Let the fat cool until it is still in liquid form but not hot.

❖ Strain the fat through a cheesecloth-lined mesh strainer.

TALLOW is rendered beef, veal, or lamb fat. It is used mainly commercially to make animal feed, soap, and cosmetics, or for cooking. McDonald's managed to piss off a lot of vegetarians a while back by cooking their fries in tallow without informing the public—no wonder they were so addictive after a long night of drinking. We use lamb fat in our chicken sausages to get that rich, decadent taste that you just can't get from plain old chicken. And we also know hunters who add lamb fat to their venison burgers for a more fatty, luscious taste.

Part of nose-to-tail butchering is coming up with uses for fat, which makes up roughly 15 percent of an animal's body weight.

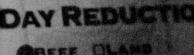
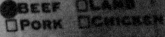

STOCK

For us, using everything means making dog food and tallow-based soap, but it also means making stock. When customers ask us to break down a whole chicken for them, we always urge them to take home the backbone and make stock. We love stock and sell lots of every kind—from duck to pork. Seeing homemade stock in a butcher's case is a good sign that they are getting whole carcasses or at least some large primals and doing their own cutting. What else are they going to do with those bones?

Homemade stock is easy to make. We prefer flavorful dark ones made by roasting bones in a 300°F oven until they are golden brown, about 1 hour (the timing will depend on the amount of bones and your oven). Don't scorch the bones or your stock will be bitter. Let cool to room temperature. Then put them in a stainless-steel pot with nothing but water (we use about 1 quart per pound of bones). Make sure the water is cold; this helps to dissolve the collagen in the bones, resulting in a richer, gelatinous stock. Bring the water to a boil, then lower to a simmer. A rolling boil will make a stock cloudy. At the shop, we simmer our stocks for up to 24 hours and even 3 days for our reductions. The longer a stock simmers, the more flavor and body is extracted from the bones. At home, simmer the stock for 4 to 6 hours, skimming off and discarding any impurities that froth on top as you go. Keep a close eye on the level of liquid in the pot. Your goal is to end up with 1 quart less liquid than what you started with. If it's evaporating too quickly, partially cover the pot, or add more water. Use in everything.

Seeing homemade stock in a butcher's cases is a good sign that they are getting whole carcasses or at least some large primals and doing their own cutting.

YOU MIGHT NOT BE READING ENTIRE CARCASSES and making candles in your kitchen, but some of what we do here in the shop can be done by anyone interested in doing basic fabricating—like cutting or tying—at home. Breaking down whole animals (see page 113) on your dining room table might be a stretch for some, but you can make sausage (see page 146), butterfly a leg of lamb (see page 123), and wrap anything for the freezer like a pro (see page 101). Once you sample your own bresaola (see page 180) or prosciutto (see page 143), you just might wind up apprenticing with us.

We have trained our fair share of butchers here—from Culinary Institute of America students to the writer Julie Powell. It doesn't matter if you are going to pen a book about your time with us (as Julie did in *Cleaving: A Story of Marriage, Meat, and Obsession*) or if you are a professional chef; either way we're going to start you out on lamb necks. Everyone starts on lamb necks.

And we suggest this is where you start at home as well. We do this because the curves and dips of whole necks make you very aware of the tip of your knife, not the length of the blade. When you're cutting, you use only the first ½ inch of the knife tip. You put your energy into the tip. It is an extension of your forearm, your hand, your wrist, your fingers. Working with necks trains you to handle what is to come, not to plunge into muscle. Once students butterfly them out nicely, then we know they are ready for the next step. (We use their results for stews and sausage.)

Small knives give you less steel to focus on. I can and do cut anything with a 5-inch knife. The length of the knife shouldn't hinder your ability to cut. I have yet to do it, but what I really want to do is take apart a pig with a pocketknife. An 8-inch slicing knife is good for stew meat and "faith" cuts (when you trust that you know where the seam or joint you're aiming for is and go right through the flesh to it), and for getting deeper in. Most of a butcher's work is boning, seaming, peeling stuff back. When students first get their hands on a knife, I tell them that they need to hold it as if someone is going to try to take it away from them. I have

them feel the balance of it, be aware of how sharp it is, be aware of where their opposite hand is. To give students an idea of how to hold a knife, I made up a couple of names: the pistol grip and the surgeon grip (see page 77). Neither of these grips are how you would hold a chef's knife, so forget everything you learned on the Food Network and pretend you are about to stab someone in the heart—there, now you've got the pistol grip down.

When it comes to handles, I'm a wood guy. Wood handles absorb fat after a while, like an old catcher's mitt when you oil the crap out of it. The fat creates a harmony, a marriage with your hand. Cutting is a Zen thing. Once you have some experience, you're really going by second nature and memorization, knowing where the bones are and how muscles overlay them. A small wood handle becomes one with your hand. You know when it shifts, when it changes. It's subtle. But the kids (that's what we call the apprentices) get knives with big plastic handles that give them more to hold on to and make them more aware. A plastic handle is molded so your hand can only fit on it in a couple of different ways. It also has a knob/guard to prevent your hand from slipping down, but of course it still can. Fat is slippery

I have yet to do it, but what I really want to do is take apart a pig with a pocketknife.

stuff. You have got to keep your handle clean.

No matter how badly students want to cut when they come to our shop to train, after I hand them their knives and before they touch them to lamb, they seize up. There is a fear of the carcass. They're afraid to grab hold of it and stick the knife in and drag it across the bone. *It's dead. You're not going to hurt it. It's fine.* They have to learn that cutting is a very physical activity. They get tired. They'll build muscles in areas where they're not used to having them. Their shoulders, neck, and head will ache. So will their legs from being on their feet all day long. Their bodies will adapt to it. Want to know what it feels like? Roll up some carpet and run around the block with it a couple of times. Carry it up some stairs. Then spend a day standing up, bent over, concentrating deeply. In the cold. With your fingers in freezing flesh. And try not to cut yourself.

This is why we have some simple rules at the shop, including Cut away from yourself. I'll say that again: Cut away from yourself. Also: Never try to catch a falling knife, and No cutting past 4:30 p.m. We start at around eight in the morning, and by the afternoon we are just too tired to cut. We don't want accidents, but cuts happen. And we're not afraid to ridicule people for being stupid with a knife. We'll send a picture of your hospital bracelet out on Twitter. We'll call you names. Just ask Four Stitch Nick. That said, everyone poops and everyone cuts themselves—us included. A few years back we were trying to rock through tons of beef when I broke two cardinal rules: it was past 4:30 and I was cutting an arm chuck, going toward me, and basically punched myself with the tip of my knife. It landed right on top of my rib and went in maybe ⅛ of an inch. It happened so fast. I pulled it out, pinched the skin really hard, and had one of the guys wrap me up. The next week people were screwing around after 4:30 again and someone put a knife in his arm. I don't make the rules because they're funny; I make them because they're necessary.

One dude who used to work for us, Aaron Lenz, wore armor when cutting. We made fun of him. The first thing Jess did after I stabbed myself was to call him and find out where he got it; she bought eight pairs. Now everyone at the shop wears a metal mesh apron. Thank you, Aaron. Jessica wanted me to go to the hospital, so I did. It turns out I was really lucky. Had my knife gone in between my ribs, I could have bled out internally. Or if it had plunged into the soft part under my rib cage, I could have died of sepsis. My scar is an inch long. I tell this story to our apprentices when I hand them their armor for the first time. You have to be careful. After they get over their fear of

HOME FABRICATION

To carve at home, follow these basic suggestions. They're good for lamb, poultry, beef, pork, and whatever else you bring into your kitchen that needs to be cut up.

❖ Do not cut after you've come home from a ten-hour workday. Do it on a weekend when you have time and are rested. This is not a testosterone-driven race against the clock.

❖ Set yourself up and put everything in its place before you start cutting: your knife or knives and steel. This is what the French call *mise en place*. A damp rag put under the cutting board (we prefer wood) will keep it sturdy, so it doesn't move around. Have towels around for wiping your hands.

❖ Know where your kids are—short ones, in particular, since they are eye level with the knife tip.

❖ Always know where your opposite hand is. The worst cuts happen to your opposite hand, not your arm or your chest.

❖ Clean up as you go. Don't let your knife get too slippery; stop to wash and dry it as needed.

❖ If you cut yourself, put your knife down in a secure place, go over to the sink, and wash the wound out. We use oregano oil and tea tree oil as antiseptics. Use triple antibiotic ointment for bad cuts, especially if you were cutting chicken, pork, or aged meat. Bandage the cut well and cover it with a plastic glove if needed before proceeding.

meat, and after they master lamb necks, they have to make their way through the rest of the lamb before I let them near a pig or—what everyone lusts for—a steer.

TOOLS OF THE TRADE

If you want to cut meat, you're going to need the following:

Knives

The blades you use to chop vegetables don't work for raw meat. In the shop, we train our apprentices on the same three knives we recommend for cutting meat at home: a 5-inch stiff boning knife, an 8-inch stiff slicing knife, and a 12-inch butcher knife. A stiff blade gives you more control than one that is flex or semiflex. A boning knife is used for what it sounds like—removing meat from bones. People really like to fetishize knives, but at the shop we're not looking for Japanese precision. We want something basic, competitively priced, and with a blade that can hold a decent edge and be honed quickly on a steel (see page 79). And by "competitively priced" we mean cheap—the blades are punched out, not forged. For novices, plastic handles are safer than wood. You do not need to spend a million bucks on these: $100 is more like it—for all three. Brands don't matter.

That said, there are some knives I do fetishize: old ones. We have a bunch of antiques hanging on the walls in the shop. People have come in and literally handed me their family butcher knives, happy to give them to a working butcher. One guy even gave me a printout of his knives' history. They belonged to a man who, like my grandfather, had a kosher butcher shop in Brooklyn. He was born in 1912 in Poland, the son of a ritual slaughterer,

and survived the concentration camps during World War II because of his skills as a trained butcher. (He removed gold teeth from corpses.) I love these knives and their backgrounds. I collect old knives, too. I find them in random places. They may not come with documents like those Brooklyn knives, but the history you can read in them is amazing. If you place old knives next to the new ones, you can see that the blades are worn away to almost nothing.

HOW TO HOLD A KNIFE

Everyone grabs his or her knife in a different way. The reality is that as you cut through an animal, you switch your grip as you go, depending on whether you are pulling a tenderloin off a drop loin or removing a brisket from an arm chuck. Here are two basic grips my hand returns to over and over again, the ones I always share with our apprentices.

THE PISTOL GRIP Wrap four fingers around the handle or hilt of your knife; this enables you to concentrate on the tip of the blade or to quickly shift the focus of your energy to the hilt or handle. Flex your wrist accordingly to change that energy and do everything from plunging the knife between the ribs of a pig to pulling the knife cleanly through a chest bone.

THE SURGEON GRIP Here you're holding the knife more like a scalpel: your index finger should cover the top of the blade, allowing you to guide it with more precision. This grip allows the finer movements you need to do things like remove the skirt from the side of a rib loin.

Steel (and Stone)

There are two things that need to happen to maintain a knife: sharpening and honing. In the most basic sense, sharpening involves removing metal from a worn blade and reshaping its edge. Unless you're a die-hard home cook, and possibly even if you are, sharpening is best done by professionals on a stone or a machine that abrades the blade, at least once a year. If you would rather not outsource the job, watch a few online videos of skilled knife grinders so you know what you're doing before you take metal off your blade.

Honing, however, is easy to do at home using a steel, which is the tool that looks like a short, squat fencing foil—sometimes it's round, sometimes flat. Because honing makes the knife cut better, it's often mixed up with sharpening. Honing is like pool rules: You always chalk a cue before shooting a ball. I never use a knife without first honing it by passing it over my steel. The cutting edge of a knife basically has microscopic teeth on it. These get dull and bent out of place with use. Honing the edge on a steel polishes and straightens it, bringing those little teeth from dullness back to life. At the shop, when we feel our knives starting to drag, we take out our steels and run our blades along them. Depending on how often you're cutting meat at home, you should hone your knives once a week or once a month, more often if you are cutting bone. I do it all day long. You need to get to know your knife and then hone it as often as you feel it needs it; there is no hard-and-fast rule.

Steels come in different lengths and different grits, or grains. The longer the steel, the more surface area you have to work with, and the coarser the grit, the "sharper" the knife will become. At the shop we have steels with different levels of grain, and we often start out with a coarse-grained steel and then touch up our knives as the day progresses with a finer grit. This is, of course, overkill at home. There, we suggest an unridged, or flat, steel with a medium- or fine-grit surface. The grit can be made of different materials: ceramic, borosilicate (a type of glass), or diamond (our favorite). It's time to sharpen your knives when honing no longer brings an edge back to them.

If you don't hone your knife, it will be like using a chain saw instead of a polished sword to cut meat.

HOW TO HONE YOUR KNIVES

You don't have to spend a huge amount of money on a steel. Whatever type of steel you're using—round ridged, round smooth, flat—you are aiming for a nice, straight angle and long, fluid, consistent movement. If you don't hone your knife, it will be like using a chain saw instead of a polished sword to cut meat.

❖ Hold the steel out in front of you, pointing up.

❖ Put the part of the knife blade closest to the handle (the widest part) flat against the top of the upright steel, then turn it so the blade is at a 20-degree angle to the steel. Slide the knife from the top of the steel to the bottom, moving it so that the entire blade from the hilt to the tip comes in contact with the steel with each stroke. Then hone the other side. Use your wrist. Take your time. Repeat five times on each side.

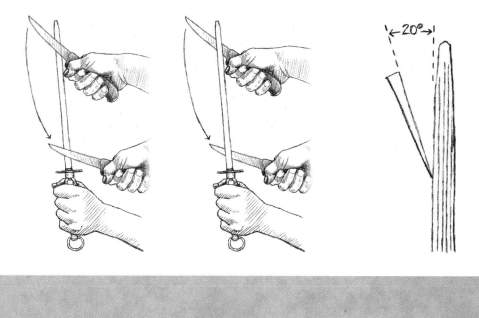

Cleaver

The cleaver is the tool everyone associates with a butcher, but it isn't actually used much in a modern butcher shop. It's archaic, not as functional as the band saw we use to buzz through bone. Band saws require less effort and cut cleaner because they don't shatter bone. Still, a cleaver has its time and place: use it to break up cooked and raw foods, especially chickens. And there's something to be said about a cleavered veal or pork chop—it's rustic. Cleavers come in all shapes and sizes, so choose one that fits your pocketbook, your lifestyle, and your kitchen drawers. Because a cleaver is used to whack through soft bone and tissue (cleaving through marrow bones is an especially dangerous maneuver), look for one that has some heft to it and that rests comfortably in your hand. Having a particularly fine or sharp edge is not as important as weight, because you are using it to crush bone and muscle, not slice cleanly.

Handsaw/Bone Saw

Most of the restaurants we sell wholesale to don't have band saws; instead, they use handsaws to get through bone—they're essential to any type of carcass breakdown. Handsaws are great for the home, too. You need a real saw, not a hacksaw, which is too small and too weak to cut through bone. Don't shop for it at a hardware store; go to a camping store or store that sells gear for deer hunters. Major knife manufacturers now make small bone saws, and these will also do the trick. Do not use your saw for anything other than cutting meat: you don't want wood or metal residue in your dinner. Change your blades often and make sure that the teeth are heading in the right direction when you do it. I've made that mistake more than once and had a hell of a time figuring out why I couldn't cut through bone as easily as I usually do.

Grinder and Hand Stuffer

So you want to make sausage. We understand. You're going to need a grinder—using a food processor instead is far from ideal. To take on pounds of sausage (see page 146), you need the right gear, like a KitchenAid electric stand mixer with a grinder attachment. If you're using casings instead of making patties, you will also need a small hand stuffer. You want the meat to remain as cool as possible throughout the process. Because it's not mechanized, a hand stuffer doesn't heat up like a KitchenAid does. You can buy one that stuffs 3 pounds at once for well under $100. If you do use a food processor, keep everything—the meat and the blades—well chilled. And pulse your meat very quickly. For a pound of 1-inch chunks of beef or lamb, the process should take only about 1 minute. Pulse on and off like you would when making pastry dough. Repeat until the meat starts to form a mass, scraping down the sides of the bowl occasionally with a spatula to move larger pieces to the bottom. A food processor makes a denser grind than a stand mixer or hand grinder and will consequently make a harder, weightier meatball, sausage, or burger when cooked. The longer you chop, the denser your grind will be, so go easy on the pulse button.

Cutting Boards

We prefer wood cutting boards to plastic ones. Wood has antimicrobial properties, doesn't dull our knives, and lasts forever. We scrape our wood table daily with a dough scraper and have it professionally sanded down yearly. Plastic, on the other hand, doesn't last; you have to throw it out when it gets grooves. Plastic is expensive and cannot always be recycled. The health department inspectors who come into the shop never have anything to say about the wood, but they always look long and hard at the cut lines in the separate plastic boards we keep for chicken and cheese. We are legally required to disinfect our shop's boards—plastic or wood—with a very weak bleach solution. At home, we prefer to use hot, soapy water; you can use the same weak bleach solution in your kitchen, or even something more people- and eco-friendly, like undiluted hydrogen peroxide (the 3 percent drugstore versions work just fine), lemon, or vinegar. If you have been prepping chicken, turn to page 200 for poultry-specific cleaning suggestions including bleach solution proportions. To clean and deodorize wooden boards, scrub them with something abrasive, like coarse salt. At the shop, we salt our table nightly to draw out moisture and impurities. This method has been used for centuries—salt has antibacterial properties and is a natural way to clean

your boards without using chemicals. Depending on how much meat you cut at home, you can get away with salting once a month, but always salt after cutting chicken. Start by slightly dampening the board, then sprinkle a fine layer of sea salt or kosher salt on it. Let it sit overnight and wipe it off in the morning. You can clean plastic boards in the dishwasher, where wood can never go. Dinged-up plastic boards should be replaced.

String

Have a spool of untreated cotton butcher's twine on hand: you don't want to use mint dental floss to tie your chicken legs together. If twine is 30 ply, that means there are thirty strands in the thread. You don't really need twine that thick, but the thicker it is, the less often it breaks. At the shop, we generally use thinner twine, like 22 ply, because I'm cheap and because I know what I'm doing.

SILVER CHAINS

Silver skin is a tough membrane that encloses muscles. It can surround any muscle in an animal's body, but it is more pronounced on some than others. It is particularly noticed (and reviled) on the tenderloin because cooking methods like searing or roasting cause the silver skin to become hard and unpalatable. Many retail stores leave the silver skin as well as the chain (the connective tissue that attaches the muscle to the bone—it is easily severed) on their tenderloins. Both are tough and should be removed. There are many ways to remove silver skin; none are wrong, but using a short knife helps to control your slicing. Remember, the goal is to always leave as much meat on the muscle while removing all of the skin.

Dough Scraper

We use a metal pastry scraper to shave fat residue and other scraps off the butcher block nightly. It can work on your wooden cutting board, too.

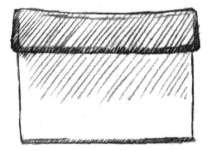

Scabbard

Scabbards are to butchers what tool belts are to carpenters: we wear them to hold our knives. They are made of plastic, leather, or metal. At the shop, we use aluminum ones. They come apart easily for cleaning and aluminum is relatively soft so it doesn't dull the knives.

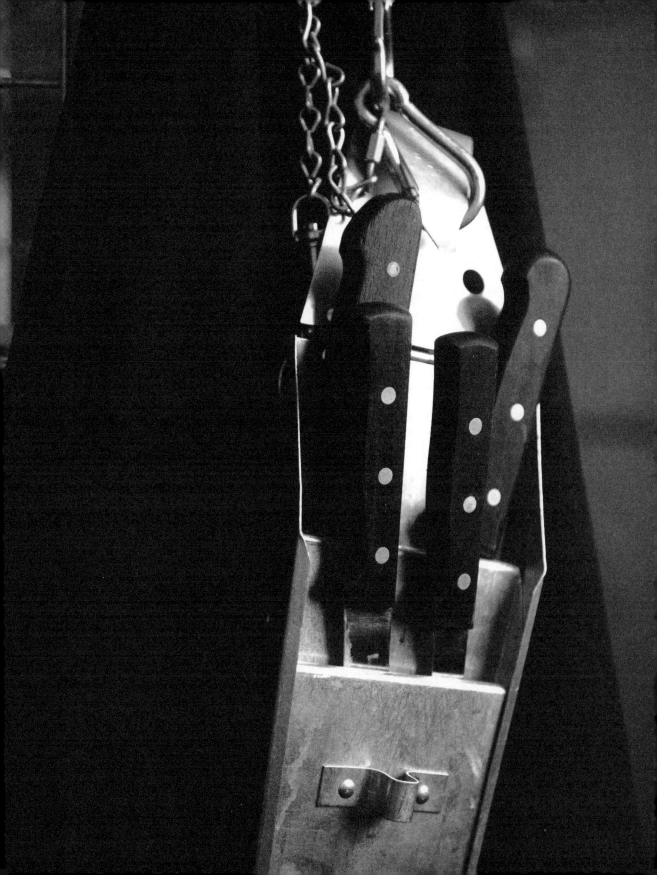

Chain Mail

Everyone wants to wear chain mail when they first get to the shop; along with the scabbard it imbues a certain butcheryness that gives you a real swagger. The chain-mail aprons weigh 4 to 5 pounds each. With the scabbard, knives, and chain belts that hold aprons on, we are so loaded down that it's a relief to get these things off at the end of the day. The bigger relief though is knowing that our chests, groins, and upper thighs are protected as we cut—one nick of the femoral artery and you can bleed out in minutes. There are also cut gloves made of mesh and arm guards to protect the arm you are *not* cutting with.

> Everyone wants to wear chain mail when they first get to the shop; along with the scabbard it imbues a certain butcheryness that gives you a real swagger.

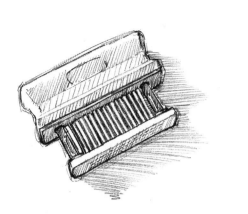

Jaccard Meat Tenderizer

If you bang meat with a mallet in an effort to tenderize it, all you're really doing is flattening it. Why assault a steak? Do you want to kill it twice? A Jaccard meat tenderizer does the trick for notoriously chewy steaks (top round, flat iron, eye round, sirloin tip) without the violence. It has forty-eight flat needlelike blades (round ones will puncture flesh and make it bleed out). You press it down into the steak, sending those needles directly into the flesh. This shortens the muscle fibers, making the meat much more tender. It's great for pastured animals, which often need a little extra tenderizing. It also makes marinades work faster, as they can penetrate deep into the flesh. The jaccard's design also means it doesn't mash up the meat; it still looks like steak. It's so genius that the old-timer who first turned me on to it told me to keep it a secret, and to keep my back to customers when I used it so it seemed like my own personal magic. Do not use it on skirts, flanks, hangers, or any money meats that don't need its powers. If you overdo it, your steak will taste prechewed. For a large 2- to 3-pound top round, I do it ten to fifteen times all over the steak; for a small flat iron, I use it six times, changing patterns to shorten the fibers in different ways.

Hook

Unless you're a hunter, it's not likely you'll be using a metal hook at home. We barely use them in the shop and only on beef. Working with gravity, hooks are used for tearing—you hook the tail end of a sirloin tip or the edge of a shoulder clod. You can also use it to scrape bones to clean them, sort of like a dentist. The hook is not for the faint of heart.

Meat Thermometer

This is one of the most useful kitchen tools to have. We use ours all the time and always tell customers to cook a steak or a burger to a certain temperature rather than attempting to time it. You should absolutely own a meat thermometer. There are many different types to choose from: they range from the cheap kind that you insert into the meat when you take it out of the oven to more expensive probes that you leave in while cooking. Some even have timers that notify you when the meat has reached a certain temperature. A dial or a digital display is up to you (and your wallet). The only ones we don't approve of are the type that have the temperature readings for beef, pork, lamb, or poultry on the face of the thermometer itself; their standardized interior temperature ranges mean you are destined to overcook your dinner.

When using a meat thermometer, insert it into the thickest part of the meat, but do not hit the bone. Look for a temperature of 5 degrees below the "actual" final temperature you're going for; meat continues to cook at least that much after you have removed it from a heat source. Wash your thermometer with hot soapy water after every use—never put it in the dishwasher.

COOKING

Pastured animals are different from conventionally raised animals in every way imaginable. So, of course, they need to be cooked differently, too (unless you want to overcook some great meat). These free-ranging animals spend time outside roaming around and developing muscles. Factory-farm animals hardly move, and some never live life outside of cages: they have that flaccid, flabby thing going on—no muscle definition. For the most part, pastured meat cooks faster because it has less fat to protect it. In addition, factory-farm meat is often injected with a saline brine that not only adds flavor and weight but also increases cooking time. You don't need to be a fancy cook to handle pastured meat, but knowing a few techniques and being aware of which ones to use for various cuts will make a world of difference. Before you start, get to know your oven and your stovetop. Is your oven convection, or standard gas or electric? Do you know how to use it? How accurate is your oven? Is the 425°F called for in a recipe actually 425°F in your oven? Knowing how your equipment responds will help you achieve the best cooking results.

Is It Done?

To avoid overcooking pastured meat, use a meat thermometer to check for doneness as you cook. Don't go by the manufacturer's temperature guide written on the thermometer; instead, follow our guidelines (see page 90). You can also test doneness by doing the hand test.

THE HAND TEST Poke the center of the meat (the least cooked area) with your fingertip. The more rare it is, the more tender it will be and the less bounce back the muscle will have.

❖ If the center feels squishy like the space around the base of your thumb or between your thumb and pointer finger, it's rare.

❖ If the center feels like the heel of your relaxed hand, it's medium.

❖ If the center feels like the heel of your flexed hand, it's well-done.

❖ If the center feels like the tip of your nose, it's overcooked.

Techniques

Our favorite way to cook almost anything is to pan-sear and oven-finish it. (We refer to this method as "stovetop to oven" throughout this book. See the tip on page 95 for the best pans to use.) It's a restaurant technique that not only keeps meat juicy but also puts a nice crust on it. But there are other ways to get dinner on the table.

Fleisher's

GRASS-FED & ORGANIC MEATS

PORK / LAMB / CHICKEN / BEEF

STOVETOP TO OVEN READY PAN (ALL METAL)

1. OVEN PREHEAT 300° (10 MINUTES)

2. HEAT PAN ON STOVETOP TO SMOKING POINT

3. PRE-SALT EACH SIDE (5~10 MINUTES AHEAD OF TIME)

4. PUT INTO PAN / SEAR FOR 2 MINUTES EACH SIDE

5. PUT PORK/LAMB/CHICKEN/BEEF INTO OVEN W/PAN

6. PORK > 6 MINUTES UP TO 10 MINUTES IN OVEN (125°)

   LAMB > 4~8 MINUTES IN OVEN (120°)

   CHICKEN > 10~15 MINUTES IN OVEN (135°~140°)

   BEEF > 4~8 MINUTES IN OVEN (120°)

7. TAKE OUT OF OVEN—LET SIT (REST) FOR 5 MINUTES

8. enjoy! ♡ Josh ♡

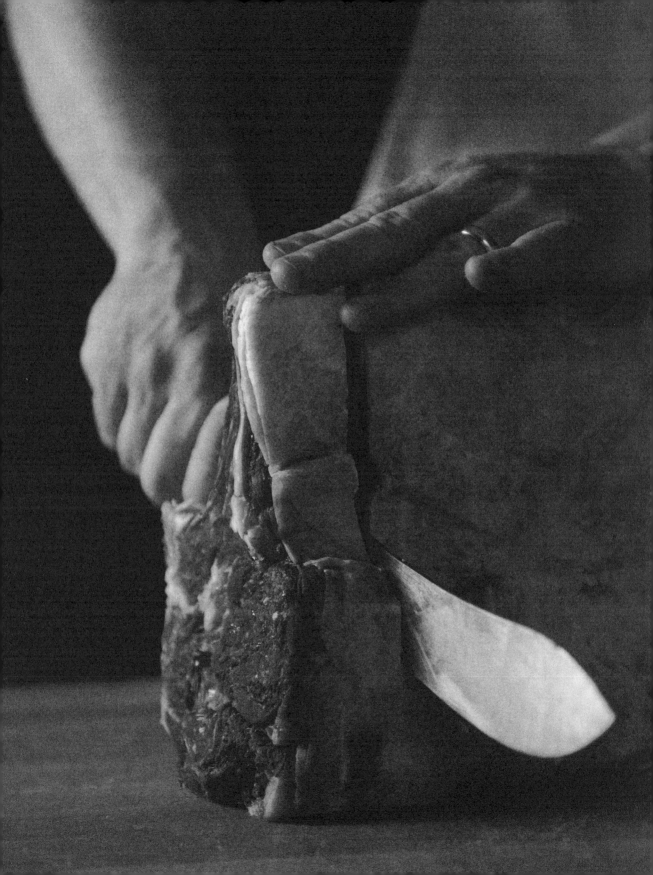

STEAKER SHOCK

People often complain that grass-fed and organic meat (and everything else organic) is too expensive, that they can't afford it, that it's not for them, or that it's elitist. We firmly believe that well-raised meat is for everyone. If you share any of these concerns, first consider the amount of meat you eat—generally Americans buy and eat too much meat. You don't need mountains of sausages or pounds of ground beef to make a sauce. Reduce portion sizes. It's better for you, and it will make well-raised meat affordable. If you would like to try something like filet but can't get over the sticker shock, buy ¼ pound of it and don't make it the centerpiece of your meal. Beyond eating less and shrinking portion size, you can also lower costs by buying cheaper cuts instead of rib eyes and strips. And plan for leftovers—a big roast can be dinner tonight and sandwiches tomorrow. If you buy smart and cook smart, you can make up the price difference between conventional and pastured meat. When people say our prices are too high, Jess invites them to throw $50 on the counter and watch her work. She can get them ten meals for half a bill. When she first made the claim, I must admit even I didn't believe her. But she proved me wrong.

TEN MEALS FOR HALF A BILL

Here is Jessica's list of ten quick, delicious, easy-to-prepare meals for four. The meat costs only $50 and change. If you don't eat meat every day, that means enough meals for two weeks.

1. **Ground beef** (½ pound) $3
Beef and Bean Enchiladas

2. **Bacon** (¼ pound, or about 3 slices) $3
Collard Green and Black-Eyed Pea Soup

3. **More bacon and eggs** (¼ pound, or about 3 slices, and three eggs) $5
Spaghetti alla Carbonara

4. **Sausages** (¾ pound, or 3 sausages) $6
Chinese Broccoli with Sausage and Polenta

5. **Chicken thighs** (1 pound) $5
Thai Chicken Stir-fry with Vegetables

6. **Pork stew meat** (1 pound) $8
Quick Pork and Chile Stew with Hominy

7. **Stir-fry beef** (½ pound) $4.50
Stir-fry Beef with Rice Noodles

8. **Whole chicken** (3 to 4 pounds) $12
Roast Chicken

9. **Eggs** $4
Frittata

10. **Roast chicken bones** $0
Chicken Soup

BAKE Putting meat in the dry heat of an oven at a fairly low temperature—below 325°F or so—works best if you have calibrated your oven. It also works best with added sauce or with meats that have been brined so they won't dry out, like chicken thighs in tomato sauce, a ham, or even a meat loaf. If you aren't using sauce, try placing a dish of water in the oven. It acts almost like a steamer, adding moisture.

BRAISE To break down muscle and get deep flavor, brown the meat, then cook it tightly covered in liquid on low heat for a long time. You can braise in the oven or on the stovetop. We love to braise pig cheeks or brisket.

BROIL We think of broiling as a finishing technique only. It's great for crusting cheese on top of your onion soup, or melting blue cheese on your open-face roast beef sandwich.

GOING AGAINST THE GRAIN
We would never caution you about what to do in your personal life, but when it comes to cutting meat always go against the grain. Muscle fibers line up in all meat to form a grain, and when you cut meat—raw or cooked—you always want to go against it. Otherwise the muscle shrinks and toughens when uncooked or becomes stringy and even tougher when cooked.

GRILL Like lots of people, we really love to grill meat. But we cannot tell you how often we hear from customers who burn their steaks because they walk away to open a beer, weed their garden, or whatever. There is no difference between a stove and a grill: You wouldn't walk away from something on the former and you shouldn't walk away from something on the latter. Stand over it. Get to know your grill, whether gas or charcoal. Grease it before you grill. When you start your grill, be sure to set up a hot side and a cold side so that you can move your meat from one side to the other without the risk of burning it. Use the top racks to slow(er)-cook meats you have seared. Read a little on the subject so you know the difference between barbecuing, smoking, and grilling.

POACH Simmering chicken breast or sweetbreads gently in liquid (usually stock) on the stovetop just below the boiling point can result in soft, tender flesh. This technique often works well for delicate cuts, but it's not our favorite.

ROAST Temperature is the difference between baking and roasting. Both happen in the oven, but roasting is done at 350°F and up, give or take. Loins, chickens, chops, steaks—we roast them all.

SAUTÉ A large, shallow pan with a small amount of melted fat, butter, oil, or lard,

HOW TO TIE A ROAST

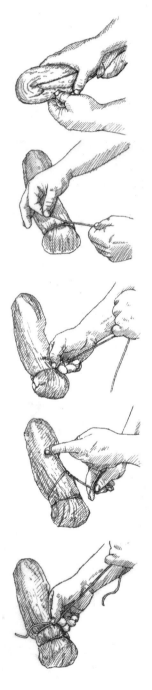

Tying a roast creates even density so that it cooks consistently and is easier to handle. Doing it right means all parts cook (more or less) evenly. There are many ways to tie, including one-handed techniques. People can get pretty obsessive about how well they tie, but for me it's all about making it look nice for the case. The knots have to be tight, they have to line up orderly and neat, and there can't be a lot of wasted twine. At home, just tie it. It doesn't matter what it looks like; there is no award. If you know how to tie your shoes, then I can teach you how to tie a roast.

❖ Get your twine. To use the least amount of it, unwind it continually off the spool as needed rather than cutting it before you tie the knots.

❖ Start at one end of the roast and work toward the other. Run the twine back and forth underneath the meat as it sits on the cutting board before you start to tie. This moistens the twine so it will stretch and not snap.

❖ One end of the roast may be thinner. That's the nature of the business. If possible, tuck the thinner ends under, as on a full tenderloin, and tie so the roast is of an even density.

❖ The goal is to make loops—evenly spaced by an inch or so—until you've tied the whole roast. However you get there is up to you—if you know how to make fancy knots go for it, just make sure you pull them *tight* until you see bulges.

❖ When you're done, the roast should look like the Very Hungry Caterpillar after he ate too much.

placed over relatively high heat, is the perfect vehicle for sautéing cutlets, thinly sliced steaks, liver, and sweetbreads and other offal. Sautéing is a quick cook so larger chops and steaks won't work with this method.

SEAR We like to sear—quickly cook on high heat—certain cuts of meat that are thin. (We pan-sear and then oven-finish thicker cuts.) Searing creates a nice crust on the outside and a juicy interior, though it does not "lock in the juices" as many

people believe. This method, which uses little or no fat in the cooking process, is especially good for cutlets and minute steaks.

STIR-FRY This extremely quick method of cooking is usually done in a wok. Both meat and vegetables are cut up into relatively equal sizes to ensure that everything cooks all at once. Little oil is needed but constant movement is necessary; always shake the wok or keep stirring the food to prevent burning or sticking.

Rub Your Meat

We often eat our meat with nothing more than salt. But sometimes extra flavor is called for. You can add some with a rub—spices, herbs, sugar, and sometimes a little liquid—applied to the meat a few hours before cooking. A rub not only imparts flavor but also helps form a crust. It's the sage-infused rub that makes our rotisserie chicken what it is (see page 216). We also rub our pork ribs with a great classic barbecue mixture (see page 153). Marinades are liquid plus herbs, spices, garlic, and onions. What kind of liquid depends on the recipe, or is up to you. Oils are the key base, then add wine, beer, lemon juice, vinegar, or even yogurt to tenderize. Keep in mind that acids break down muscle: marinades containing acids shouldn't be left sitting for more than twelve hours. Marinating tender cuts, like a pork tenderloin, takes far less time. If you're using soy sauce, sugar, mirin, honey, agave, or maple syrup in your marinade, watch your meat carefully as you cook; the sweetness in these ingredients can cause meat to burn more easily. Marinating can be done quickly at room temperature, but if you plan on more than a half hour, do it in a pan or a sealable bag in the refrigerator. Do not reuse a marinade as a sauce.

Brines

Brining is a great thing for home cooks to do; brines keep meat moist. We brine meat that will be slow-cooked or smoked, especially pork: all of our bacon, ham, and chops are brined before being smoked. Chicken and (Thanksgiving) turkey also benefit from brining. To brine, let the meat sit in a water, salt, and sugar solution for at least 12 hours. The smaller the cut

BEYOND MEAT

It goes without saying (but we'll say it, anyway) that at the shop and at home we use local/organic ingredients— oil, soy sauce, garlic, herbs, spices, onions, lettuce, tomatillos, you name it—and suggest you do, too.

or animal, the shorter the brine time. We use a basic 3 gallons:2 cups:1 cup ratio of water to salt to sugar. We always mix our sugar and salt with a small amount of boiling water to dissolve them and then add cold water. You can play with the liquid for different flavors—cider and orange juice come to mind. If your liquid contains sugar or salt, remember to reduce the sugar or salt in your basic ratio. And keep in mind that sugars make the meat cook and caramelize a lot quicker. You can also throw in bay leaf, juniper berries,

EXCUSE ME, I OFF-GASSED

As meat ages, it off-gases, or naturally releases gases as it decomposes. If you dry-age meat (see page 168), these vapors release into the air. If you vacuum-seal it in a bag (aka wet aging; also see page 168), it stays in the plastic. So when you open the plastic, out comes a particular smell—it's sulfuric, gassy, or as we say in the shop, *farty*. The commercial meat industry pretties this up by calling it "cryobloom." Whatever you call it, it's okay. Let the meat sit out on a plate. If it still smells after twenty minutes, toss it; it's no longer good. When poultry is removed from plastic, it should be washed in cold, running water—never lukewarm or warm. Then leave it out for ten minutes before you check it. Don't wash lamb or beef; it will turn black. Though it doesn't turn dark, we suggest you don't wash pork, either.

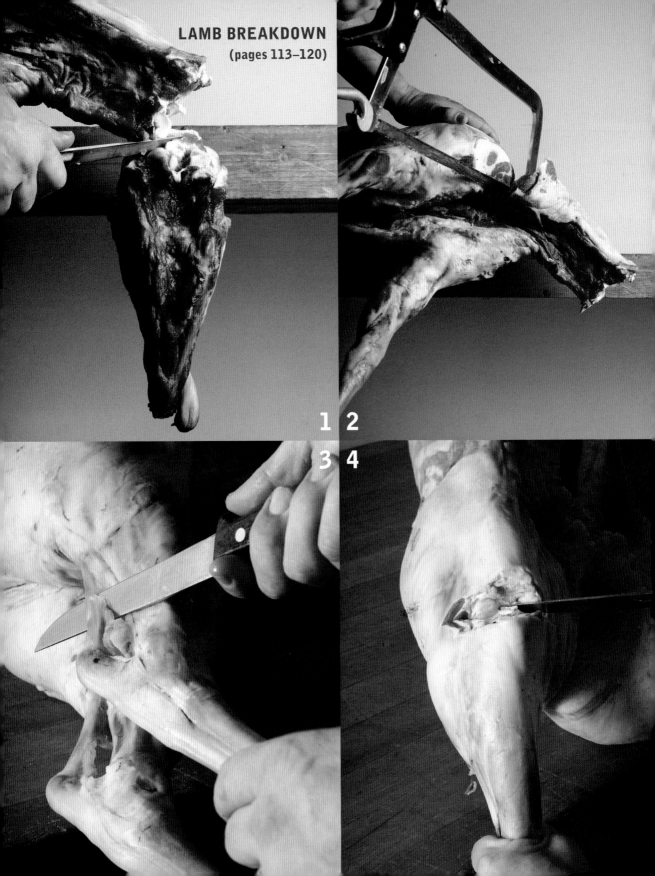

LAMB BREAKDOWN
(pages 113–120)

1 2
3 4

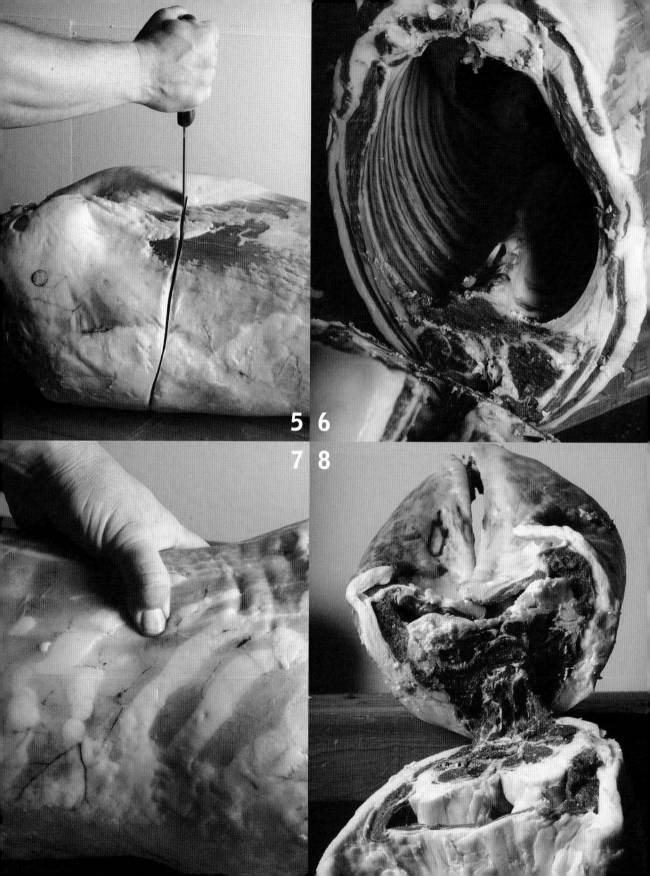

5 6
7 8

9 10
11 12

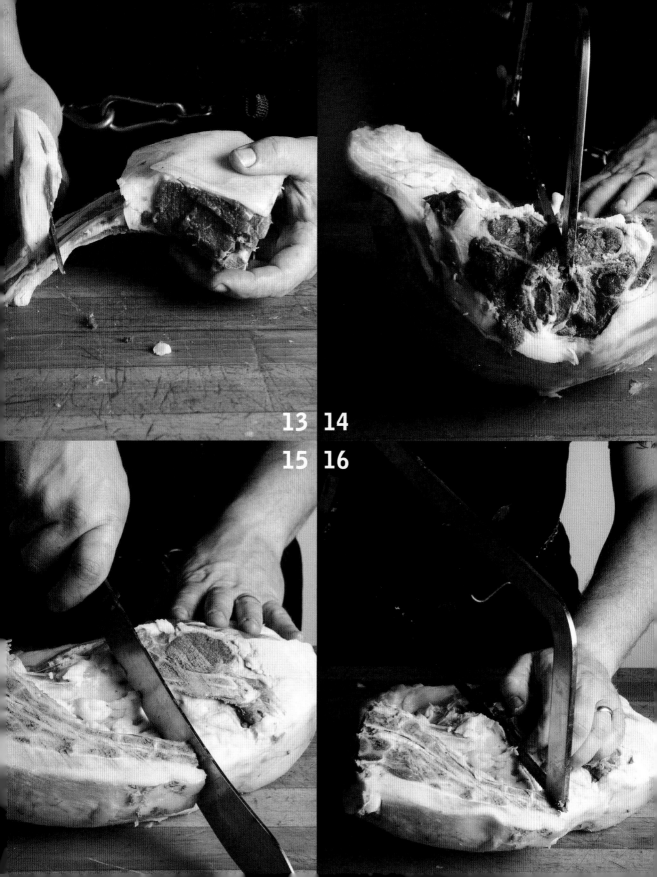

13 14

15 16

GRILLED BUTTERFLIED LEG OF LAMB
WITH INDIAN-STYLE WET RUB (page 122)

1 2
3 4

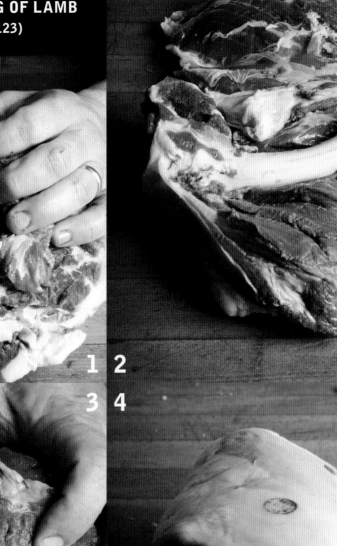

QUICK LAMB MEATBALLS
(page 121)

THE BEST PORK CHEEKS EVER
(page 140)

PIG TO PORK

Throughout the year, Fleisher's offers pig-to-pork classes—full-day events from slaughter to sausage making—in an effort to bring people closer to where their food comes from.

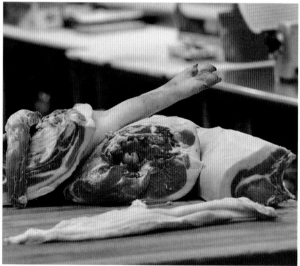

SALTS
(page 141)

FATS (page 66)

DUCK FAT

FATBACK

SALT PORK

LEAF LARD

LARD

BACON FAT

**BONE-IN BELLY=
SPARERIBS AND BACON**
(page 151)

BACON
(page 152)

DRIVEWAY PIG ROAST
(page 154)

and other herbs. At the shop, we brine in buckets in our walk-in. At home you can do it just about anywhere. A turkey brining in a stockpot might not fit in your fridge, but it does just fine in a sealed plastic bag placed in an icy cooler or—during the freezing winter—in a clean bucket or clean garbage can out on the back porch, protected from local wildlife and neighborhood pets.

GUIDE TO STORING MEAT

If you've carefully sourced your pastured meat, you will want to store it well. Follow these guidelines for fresh meat:

In the Fridge

When you get home from the butcher, loosen the wrapping around the meat, except for chicken, and put it on a plate. Rotate the meat daily to let air flow around it until you use it. Larger bone-in pieces can be kept the longest; most processed cuts and grind are good only for a few days.

BEEF

Fresh beef will keep in your fridge for

❖ 2 to 10 days if not vacuum-sealed, depending on the cut. If it has a coating and smells sour, it's done. Discard it.

❖ 2 to 3 weeks if vacuum-sealed. After that, smell check it.

PORK

Fresh pork will keep in your fridge for

❖ 2 to 7 days if not vacuum-sealed. The more air you give it, the longer it will last. If it darkens, that's okay, but if it's tacky or slimy, throw it out.

❖ 2 to 3 weeks if vacuum-sealed. After that, smell check it.

LAMB

Fresh lamb will keep in your fridge for

❖ 5 to 7 days if not vacuum-sealed. If it gets tacky, has a sour smell, or is otherwise clearly not pleasant, you should not be putting it in your mouth.

❖ 2 to 3 weeks if vacuum-sealed. After that, smell check it.

POULTRY

Fresh poultry will keep in your fridge for

❖ 4 days if not vacuum-sealed.

❖ 10 days if vacuum-sealed. Give it a rinse under cold, running water and let it sit on a clean plate uncovered for ten minutes. (It sounds obvious, but do not use soap on any meat product ever.) After that, if it smells sulfuric or sour, or if it feels tacky, immediately throw it out and clean the plate and your sink with bleach or vinegar (see page 200 for more on cleaning up after prepping poultry).

FRENCHING

There is no real point to frenching—taking the meat and the fat off the first couple of inches of bone on a rack of beef, pork, or lamb, with the chops or steaks still attached to the ribs—but it's pretty, and very butchery (especially if you put crowns on the resulting bare bones). If you can find an un-frenched rack, frenching is an excellent party trick to try at home. And if you're breaking down an entire lamb on the dining room table (see page 113), you'll absolutely want to know how to do it yourself. There are several ways to french—some people even swear by using twine to scrape the meat off the bone. We tend to use our knives. What you take off is tasty meat that we put into sausages at the shop. You can use it in a sauté or a grind, or to make the dog supremely happy.

FRENCHING USING A 5-INCH KNIFE

❖ Cut a line across the length of the rack. Use pressure; this cut should go through to the bones. Make sure you are far enough away from the meaty bits, about 1 inch from the eye, or center, of the chop. You don't want to sacrifice too much meat; you want to leave enough on the bone to gnaw on.

❖ Using just the tip of your knife, pull the fat cap away from the bones.

❖ Turn the rack so that the area where the chops reside is facing you and make a vertical cut in the center of the rack. Start to carefully peel back the thick layer of fat and meat. Work from the center out toward the ends. Turn it over, trim the other side, and remove the nerve that runs the length of the rack.

❖ Make a cut ½ inch away from the eye of the rack across the ribs. Flip the rack and repeat. Pull the meat away from the bones using the tip of your knife.

❖ Deeply score the membrane around the bones so that you will be able to use your fingers to pop the meat off the bones.

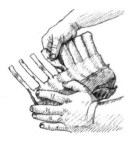

❖ Once you get the meat off the bones, clean them with your fingers, the back of your knife, or with twine. By using twine, you will get beautifully clean bones. Take a piece of string and make a semitight knot around the bone where it connects to the muscle. Pull the string toward you, removing all the fat and meat as you go. Make sure the knot is loose enough to slip easily up and down the bone and tight enough to remove the meat.

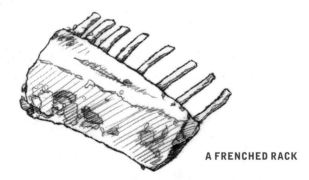

A FRENCHED RACK

How to Freeze Meat

If you are going to freeze the meat you buy, ask your butcher to vacuum-seal it. This extends the life of the meat (fresh or frozen) up to five times by removing the oxygen in the package, thereby limiting the growth of bacteria that causes meat to decompose. Cryovac is the industry term because that company produces most of the vacuum-sealing equipment on the market.

If your meat hasn't been hermetically sealed by your butcher, you'll need to wrap it. We suggest using a technique called sandwich wrapping, which calls for plastic wrap and paper (butcher paper made specifically for freezing or plain butcher wrap). The plastic keeps the meat from sticking to the paper or bleeding through it, and the paper insulates the meat, creating a barrier. Red meat turns black if it touches itself, so if you're wrapping more than one piece in a package, placing plastic sheets between them will help prevent this discoloration. Meat that is black is not bad to eat; it's just not visually pleasing.

How long frozen meat will keep depends on your freezer (what type it is and how often it was opened) and on whether the meat was vacuum-sealed, and, if not, on the skill of the person who wrapped it. If left too long in a freezer, meat can dry out and pick up odors from its neighbors. There usually isn't a safety issue unless there is a change in temperature, as when you defrost, freeze, and defrost again, which gives bacteria a chance to grow. Generally speaking, vacuum-sealed meat lasts for a year, paper-wrapped for six to eight months. Larger cuts of meat like roasts will last longer frozen, while grinds often dry out or get freezer burn after a few months. Supermarket packaging, though safe to freeze in, does not offer a tight seal and leaves the meat exposed to the air already inside the package. If you do freeze your meat this way it will retain its quality for a mere one to two months. If you rewrap it well, you will find that its shelf life is extended for up to a year.

How to Defrost Meat

The best way to defrost is to plan ahead. Take the meat out of the freezer and let it thaw on a plate in the lowest part of the fridge so it doesn't drip on anything. A turkey or a roast might need two or three days. A steak, depending on its thickness, might only require twenty-four hours. If the meat is wrapped in plastic, leave it in the plastic. If it is wrapped in paper, take the paper off if possible. If you haven't planned ahead, you can also defrost small portions of meat in a bowl of cold water. The water must remain cold. Do not defrost with warm or hot water; that's begging for food poisoning.

HOW TO SANDWICH WRAP

Generally speaking, this method will keep meat in the freezer fresh for six to eight months, depending on the skill of the wrapper.

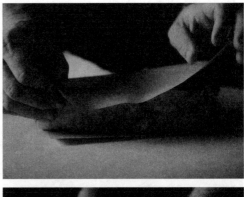

❖ Take a piece of meat and wrap it tightly in steak paper or plastic (sheet wrap is preferable to a bag; if using one, be careful to compress it and push all the air out).

❖ Place the wrapped meat in the center of a sheet of butcher paper large enough to wrap around it like a gift (about one and a half times). If the paper is coated, the shiny side should face the meat.

❖ Fold the paper in half around the meat so the ends meet. Start folding it down, pushing all the air out as you go, especially when you make the last fold.

❖ Press the paper down to seal off the sides of the meat, pushing air out as you go. Fold the two sides in.

❖ Turn the ends under the package. It should look like a bonbon/sandwich/piece of candy— whatever you want to call it, it should be airtight. Put a rubber band around it. Store with the seam side down.

❖ Label and date the package so you will know what's in there and how long you can keep it.

WE'RE PARTIAL TO LAMB, JESSICA ESPECIALLY. We love the grassiness. We love that the big bold flavor lends itself to spicing (cumin, curry, cilantro, peppers, garlic, onions) and pairs well with fruits (pomegranates and apricots come to mind) and dairy (yogurt, feta cheese), but holds its own with just salt and pepper. We even love its fat—it's creamy, subtly flavored, and the ultimate emulsifier. But out of all the meats we sell, we move the least lamb. It's just one of those things— you either love it or hate it. If it's too gamy, people freak out.

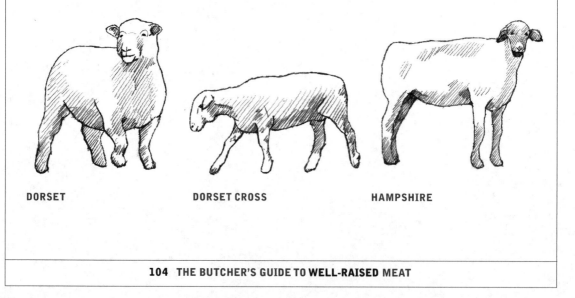

DORSET   DORSET CROSS   HAMPSHIRE

The lamb we're currently selling comes from three farms, including one run by one of our slaughterhouse guys. The animals are totally free-roaming—so much so that one farmer says he lets them go into the woods after they're born and comes back in about a year to find them. It's phenomenal. They have hundreds of acres to run on and their diet is pasture-heavy. The lambs eat grass when grass is on the ground, but they eat local unsprayed corn, too; the corn mellows out the muscle. Of course there's no "juice" ever. They usually weigh somewhere between 70 and 100 pounds, male and female. Sometimes we'll get in a 125-pounder. It's like a dinosaur. The farmer will say, "Yeah. Just found that one." Lambs are skittish, not very easy to catch. We prefer it if our farmers "find them" sooner.

When we first opened the shop, we did 100 percent grass-fed (see page 228) lamb for a while. These were smaller animals—around 60 pounds. Jess could carry one herself through the door. We loved the flavor, but they were a hard sell. They tasted "lamby." Funny how no one wants their lambs lamby. Other words we heard to describe the meat were *minerally* and even *livery*. That's no good. A little chew is good from a pastured animal, but this lamb was sometimes on the bad side of chewy. What we're selling now is much more tender. And it tastes great—lamby enough, but not too lamby. Buttery and smooth. It has a well-balanced flavor for free-foraging animals. The texture is like beef—very firm, with a good tight grain. It's also authentic: New Zealanders and Australians come in and tell us our shop is the only place where they can get lamb that tastes like lamb. And they know lamb.

BREEDS

There are many meat breeds out there, and we have sold the most common ones—Suffolks and Dorsets (both breeds are fast gainers; the Suffolk is on the large side, and the Dorset is durable), Dorset Crosses, and Hampshires (also a fast gainer, with a good meat-to-bone ratio). Our current forest-foraging animals are a basic breed cross that does well on our local farms and has a larger frame to handle more weight. Small lambs aren't very marketable. We prefer larger ones; they sell better and have a better yield.

SUFFOLK

PASTURED VS. ORGANIC VS. CONVENTIONAL

Generally speaking, lambs don't get as many drugs as other conventionally raised-for-food animals. Lambs tend to be raised outside, as they should be; ruminants belong outdoors where they can graze. Most of the lamb sold in America is not a local product; it is imported from New Zealand and Australia. These imported animals are small (that's the way Brits and Europeans like them). There's also almost no variety; it's hard to find anything but legs and loins for sale. Administering hormones to sheep is banned in New Zealand, as is routine feeding of antibiotics. Australia also outlaws "hormone-growth promotants." These restrictions seem to trick consumers into thinking that all imported lamb is "safe" or sustainable. Nothing is ever that black-and-white.

Unlike New Zealand, Australia, and many other countries, the United States permits the use of hormones in ruminants (although the American Lamb Board contends American lamb is "free of artificial growth hormones"). And, like any nonorganic animals stateside, they might also be given antibiotics. American lamb usually comes from states nowhere near our shop—Colorado, California, Wyoming, Texas, and South Dakota. The lambs we sell are fully pastured in New York's Hudson Valley. Overgrazing isn't

BY ANY OTHER NAME

EWE Female sheep that has lambed

LAMB Male or female sheep, up to one year old

MUTTON Meat from sheep older than two years

RAM Male sheep that is sexually mature, ready to go

SHEEP The animal when it's older than one year

YEARLING Male or female sheep between one and two years old

an issue because they forage. They eat all sorts of brush, and even help keep the weeds down.

Domestic organic lamb can be another good option, but it's a pretty rare product and usually is not local. Buying organic gives you a level of trust about how the animal was fed, but it doesn't guarantee much about how it was raised. Keep in mind that just because an animal is raised locally doesn't automatically mean it's free of hormones and antibiotics. You have to carefully source your meat.

BEYOND OUR BREEDS

Meat breeds sound like stops along an English train line: Shropshire, Oxford, and Southdown. It should come as no surprise then that many of them originated in Britain. The Brits love their lamb (and even enjoy mutton, a very gamy meat from sheep older than one year) and have spent many hundreds of years perfecting these breeds. To us all sheep look the same—like *merguez*—but we have a unique view of the world.

CHEVIOT
Rare in the United States, cheviots are an extremely old breed from the hill country between Scotland and England. Records show that these guys were roaming around as early as the fourteenth century. They are another dual-purpose breed, used for both wool and meat.

OXFORD
These heritage sheep have brown faces and white, thick, woolly fleeces. They produce large meaty carcasses that make them popular among lamb farmers.

SOUTHDOWN
When you imagine a sheep, this is it—soft white wool, white fuzzy face. This breed is hardy and was developed about two hundred years ago in (you guessed it!) England. Originally a dual-purpose sheep—good for both meat and wool—the breed has been altered over time to be larger and has become more popular as a meat producer.

TEXEL
This breed always looks like it's wearing a white wool sweater, with its bald white face and legs surrounded by an ample white coat. They have the reputation for being the strongmen of the sheep world, known for their remarkable muscle development and leanness.

AFTER SLAUGHTER

We get our lambs whole, nonsplit, head on. For the record, I can deadlift 205 pounds from the floor. I don't want to. I want an animal to be a weight that one person can handle. Pigs and steers—obviously—are too heavy. So lamb is the only animal that comes to the shop whole, though without their skins. The slaughterhouse sells the hides to a buyer. The animals are covered in a thick fat cap, 1½ to 2 inches, that protects the muscle. They're a sight coming through our front door. We carry the lambs right past our customers to get to the back of the store. Some people are fascinated; some are horrified; some are unfazed. Neighbors have asked us to cover them up. Moms have put their hands over their kids' eyes, hiding from them what we think is a perfectly good lesson on the origins of their dinner. The head is what seems to make most clients turn away, especially the stiff black tongue clenched between the teeth.

Love it or hate it, a whole, skinned animal is striking. But as a butcher, I'm looking beyond that to make sure the muscle is firm and a deep red color. I want it to feel fresh. There should be no smell or a slightly earthy smell, the light scent of iron from the blood. I'm checking out the bone structure—if the animal gets too big, the carcass won't dry properly. If the lambs come in too large, I ask our farmer to "take them down" smaller. (That means slaughter them.) I'm constantly gauging the consistency of the fat, which should be thick, hard, and white. I want the eyes to be clear and fresh, not slimy. The tongue should be nice and dry and feel good to the touch—almost like a snake. I look at the kidneys: they should be firm, not reeking of piss, and have good color. Butchers are like surgeons. We can see from the inside out. They can tell me anything they want to about feed and drugs, but when I get an animal on the table and open it up, if what I see doesn't match what they are saying, they're gone.

We hang the lambs in the shop's walk-in for a week, as we do for pigs and steers—it concentrates the flavor and makes the meat more tender. Depending on the time of year, demand can be so high that we might not get to hang them for this long. Around New Year's the lambs tend to come in and go right back out as racks.

Americans aren't used to lamb, so it has an air of mystery. We sell mostly rack and loin, probably because these are the cuts people are familiar with. We're working to bring back things like country-style ribs from the shoulder, especially during the winter, when all we crave are hearty, deeply flavorful stews and soups that cook for hours on the stovetop. We love turning lamb into fresh sausages; it's one of the most sustainable ways of using the whole animal. Customers (much like our apprentices) tend to be really intimidated by the bone-in neck, but it's great for stewing—and economical. We like people to buy cuts they're not used to and haven't tried before.

Beyond its versatility and rich flavor, we love lamb because it's the ultimate sustainable animal. We waste nothing. And because lamb comes to the shop as a whole animal—head on, with only the fleece removed—it never lets me forget what I'm working on. Lamb always makes me aware of what I am doing and why I am doing what I do. This is truly how meat should look.

Butchers are like surgeons. We can see from the inside out.

LITTLE LAMBS

We sell a lot of lamb around Passover and Easter. No surprise there. Legs, shoulders, and lots of shank bones. Our customers inevitably ask for spring lamb. The lambs aren't actually born in the spring—traditionally they are born in the fall and harvested in the spring. In the very early days of Fleisher's, we got grass-fed spring lambs the size of our pit bull—the chops were like small lollipops. People had no idea what to do with them; it was an eye-opener. But think about it: the lambs have barely been alive—maybe four months, tops—they don't have meat on their bones yet. The only thing you can do with something that small is to cook it whole (and yes, your oven is big enough—they are *that* small!). In our experience, only Greek and Italian clients want to do that.

One Passover/Easter season, Jessica was at the slaughterhouse picking up when she ran into a farmer who was delivering giant spring lambs. Intrigued, she asked what the animals had eaten. The farmer swore up and down they only ate grass. She pushed him and pushed him (she's hard-core when it comes to sourcing meat), and finally he said, "Occasionally I give them remnants." He had been feeding them plastic bags full of stale bread and candy from local factories! True story. Some slaughterhouse guys have confirmed that they see plastic bags and candy wrappers in the guts of animals all the time. But never in our animals.

PRIMAL PRIMER

It's standard in the industry to break the lamb into four primals per side: shoulder, rack, loin, and leg. We have also seen it broken into five primals. There are many different methods. At the shop we look at things a little differently and break down lamb into three primals: shoulder, saddle (which encompasses both the rack and the loin), and leg.

The whole *shoulder,* with the neck and the shanks—both sides—weighs 35 to 40 pounds. The shoulder runs from the first rib through the fifth rib and includes the neck and the shank. The cuts from this section are ideal for braising because this set of muscles is in perpetual motion.

The *saddle,* which runs from the sixth rib through the thirteenth rib, is made up of the rack section and the loin section. These contain the parts of the lamb that people are most familiar with: loin and rib chops. Weighing in at about 30 pounds for an entire saddle (both sides), this primal has the least meat ratio-wise, due to the heavy fat that surrounds the kidneys. But it certainly contains the costliest cuts.

The *leg* contains the sirloin, the leg, and the shank. It weighs 30 to 35 pounds for two legs, or a whole section. As opposed to a pig or a steer, a lamb is fairly young when it is slaughtered, making the leg section relatively tender.

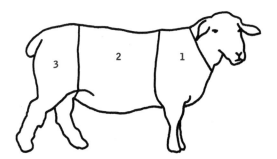

LAMB PRIMALS
1. SHOULDER
2. SADDLE
3. LEG

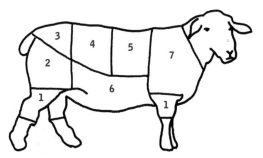

LAMB SUBPRIMALS
1. SHANK
2. LEG
3. SIRLOIN
4. LOIN (CHOPS)
5. RIB (CHOPS)
6. BELLY
7. SHOULDER

Cook This Way

SHOULDER (WITH SHANK AND NECK ATTACHED) These cuts are a Crock-Pot lover's dream.

> **Blade chops**—braise
> **Country-style ribs**—braise
> **Neck**—braise
> **Round bone chops**—braise
> **Shanks**—braise
> **Shoulder**—braise
> **Stew meat**—braise

SADDLE This most tender section provides sought-after cuts; while some cuts from the saddle are best cooked using a wet-heat method (stew meat), most respond to dry-heat methods like roasting.

> **Belly**—cure (as in "lambcetta") or grind
> **Breast**—roast or grind
> **Loin**—roast or pan-sear, then oven-finish (we call this "stovetop to oven"; see page 90)

> **Loin chops aka Porterhouse chops**—stovetop to oven or grill
> **Rack of ribs**—roast
> **Rib rack/chop**—roast or stovetop to oven or grill
> **Sausage and grind**—stovetop to oven or grill
> **Spareribs**—braise
> **Stew meat**—braise

LEG This primal features great braising and roasting cuts, but is perhaps best known for that dinner-party showstopper: a bone-in or bone-out leg; either way, roasting is best.

> **Leg**—grill or roast
> **Leg steak**—roast or stovetop to oven or grill
> **Shanks**—braise
> **Sirloin**—roast

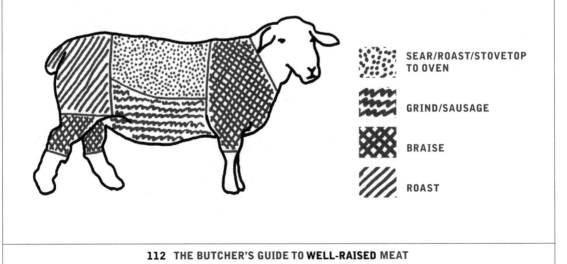

SEAR/ROAST/STOVETOP TO OVEN

GRIND/SAUSAGE

BRAISE

ROAST

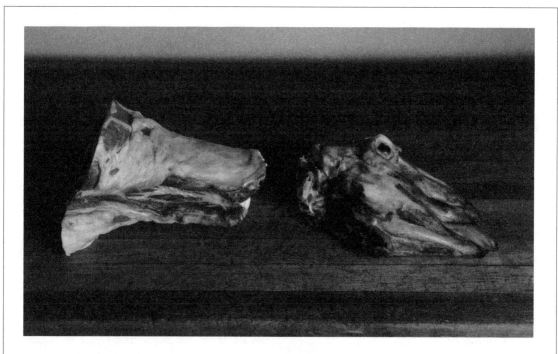

Home Fabrication

Whole lambs are perhaps the easiest of all the carcasses to break down into primals; the process takes us well under five minutes. Our apprentices are expected to be able to break down lamb before they move on to pork. Lamb is far more compact and has fewer cuts than beef or pork, which makes it an ideal animal to start on. I can butcher a lamb and have it freezer-ready in about an hour and a half, but it will take you quite a bit longer on your first attempt, so be ready to spend the day getting bloody. Breaking down a lamb carcass is also ideal because it is so similar to a deer—we train hunters on lambs, so if you hunt, this is a great skill to have.

BREAKING DOWN A WHOLE LAMB

Before you start to cut, set up a clean, well-lit space. Outside on a picnic table works well if the weather is nice and cool; indoors on your dining room table is good as long as you cover it with a huge piece of Masonite. If you are doing this at home, make sure that your wife, husband, or significant other is okay with the process before you start (if yes, he or she is either blind or a saint), because once you start there is no going back. Leave the whole day free, get your children out of the house, and make sure that the FedEx guy is not going to show up at your door. (How are you going to explain that one?)

The equipment you will need for this adventure includes:

three bins: one for trim, one for bones, one for meat

a scabbard (optional)

two knives: a 5-inch knife and an 8-inch knife

a steel

butcher's twine

butcher paper for wrapping cuts as you go

chain-mail apron

two aprons, one for under the chain mail, one for over

a handsaw

rags

Remember to clear a space in your fridge before you start so you can keep the meat you cut well chilled as you work your way through the carcass.

See the first color photograph insert for step-by-step illustrations. Boldface numbers correspond to the numbers in the insert.

Removing the Head

The first thing you want to do when butchering a lamb is to remove the head. Place the lamb on its side with the head hanging over the edge of the table so you can use the table for leverage. Flex the head up and down, looking for the atlas bone or pivoting joint. Cut straight across between the joint and the start of the vertebrae using your 5-inch knife. Use the bone as a guide for your knife. Using the tip of your 5-inch knife, de-hinge the head with a quick snap on either side of the chin and pop the head off. Retain the head for roasting if you so desire. **1**

Removing the Neck

Your next goal is to remove the neck. With your 8-inch knife, make a circular cut at the base of the neck or collarbone as if you are literally slitting someone's throat. (Imagine it's your boss.) Expose the bone with your knife, thereby laying a path for your saw. Then saw through the neck. Once you have cut through the bone you will hear a change in tone even before you see it. That is the time to switch back to your 8-inch slicing knife for a clean cut. Saws are not meant to slice through flesh just as knives are not meant to cut through bone—every tool has a very specific purpose, which is why you will find yourself switching back and forth while you are cutting. Set aside the neck to either debone for stew (see opposite) or keep on the bone for a great braise. **2**

THE BUTCHER SUGGESTS: LAMB NECK

We might be sticking *our* necks out here when we say that the neck is the most succulent of lamb cuts. The easiest, most flavorful way to cook it is to braise the entire neck and pull those meltingly delicious shards of lamb off the bone. The neck, which certainly is not a high-yield piece of meat, lends itself best to heavily spiced stews, soups, and curries, where the bits of lamb add to the melting pot of flavors. Remember that lamb neck is extremely fatty (hence the flavor), so we recommend planning ahead: leave enough time to cool your meal so that the fat congeals on the top and remove it before reheating and serving.

We start our apprentices out on lamb neck for many reasons: it's cheap, we have a lot of it, and most important, working with it teaches the new folks how to use the tip of their knives and how to flex their wrists accordingly. Cutting meat is not like cutting vegetables; you rarely use the full length of the blade as you do when slicing or julienning. You use the full range of motion of your body when you cut meat, and carrots can't teach you that. This is a different kind of precision and it requires finesse and a light touch. Necks are the perfect medium in which to gain confidence (at the shop, it's all going to be made into grind anyway).

To start, position the neck so that one end is facing you. Dig the tip of your knife into the fat on the opposite side. Draw the knife from one end to the other, dragging the tip against the bone as you go. Now, with your fingers, pry the cut open. Then, using just the top portion of your blade, slowly start separating the meat from the bone. It's like peeling an orange. The neck bones are shaped like a propeller or fan. The goal is to cut around the bones with the tip of your knife, slipping into the ridges and valleys without taking chips of bone with the meat. This is a hard process to describe but is almost instinctual once you begin. As the meat comes off the bone, make sure to clean it well of sinew, fat, and any bone chips. Beyond grinding, you can use the results as stew meat, or roll, tie, and braise it.

Another way to cut a lamb neck is to remove the two separate portions of meat from either side of the bone. Peel the flesh back in the same manner but, instead of continuing to peel, cut out one side of the neck where it is fleshiest. Then do the other side. Strip the fat from the outside and carefully remove the nuchal ligament (or as the Brits call it the paddywhack—as in "knick, knack paddywhack . . .") and the rest of the sinew. This will give you two lovely fillets that you can roast or sear. This is a very popular cut in England that has yet to make it to our shores.

Removing the Shanks: Hind and Fore

HIND SHANKS Now work on the back legs of the lamb, or hind shanks. Cut through the Achilles tendons on the hind legs to loosen the shanks, which is where the animals hang from on the hooks at the slaughterhouse or butcher shop. **3** Wiggle each leg to find the kneecap—you need to move the joint back and forth and actually grasp the joint with your fingers to see it and feel it flex to know that you are hitting the right spot when you cut. Make a small cut with the tip of your knife to make sure that you are hitting right between the two sockets. This is a very slippery area because of the synovial fluid between the joint—be careful as you cut through the joints. **4**

FORE SHANKS Next, move on to the front legs, or fore shanks. Score the front legs above the elbows just as you did with the hind shanks but break the bone with your saw. Finish the cut with the 5-inch knife. When you are cutting, remember to make only one incision at the top before you use your saw, then saw through the joint and use your knife for a nice, clean finish. Shanks are the best braising cuts around, and four good-sized shanks should feed four comfortably.

Separating the Shoulders from the Saddle

Roll the lamb onto its side and remove the kidneys and the internal fat that surrounds them (also called the kidney knob), if the slaughterhouse hasn't already done this.

Now it is time to separate the shoulders from the saddle. Lay the lamb on its back with the chest cavity pointing straight up. Gently separate the cavity with your right hand (or left, if you're a lefty) and reach into the lamb to find the first rib. Now count five ribs down. Do it again. Always count twice and cut once! Make sure you are counting from the first rib, it's difficult to find. Push your fingers as hard as you can between the ribs. Take your 5-inch knife and pierce the muscle near the spine between the fifth and sixth ribs, counting and pressing on the inside but puncturing on the outside. The knife should naturally slip between the ribs. With a quick thrust up and then down, pierce it through and pull up with all your might. **5** (Pretend you are in a prison shower scene.) Turn the lamb over and repeat on the other side. You have now separated the shoulders from the rest of the animal. **6**

Separating the Saddle from the Legs (Including Sirloin)

You now have two remaining primals to work through, the saddle and the leg. Flip the lamb onto its side. This is the hardest part of the breakdown; even seasoned butchers sometimes screw it up. Look for the section that bows in slightly before it bulges out, what we like to think of as the lamb love handles. Feel your own back first to know what you are looking for—the top of the pelvic bone. 7 Once you have located this area, make a tentative poke and once you hit the bone with the knife, move farther over, away from the rear leg. Continue to poke every millimeter or so until your knife slides through, past the bone. It is only then that you make your guide cut straight down to the spine with your 8-inch knife and start to saw. Saw through the spine until you hear the tone change from cutting bone to cutting flesh. Finish with a clean cut through the spine in the same direction you were just cutting—right through to the other side. Now the sirloin-leg combos are separated from the saddle. 8

Next is the rib-loin section, from the sixth rib through the thirteenth. Make a cut after the eighth rib and draw up and then down with full force. 9 Repeat on the other side. Hang this section over the table and saw right through the spine. 10 Now you have successfully separated the full rib rack, which contains those delectable lamb lollipops from the loin and produces delicious chops and roasts.

Congratulations! You have reduced your whole lamb into primals.

Leave the whole day free, get your children out of the house, and make sure that the FedEx guy is not going to show up at your door. (How are you going to explain that one?)

CUTTING LAMB PRIMALS INTO SUBPRIMALS

Shoulder

I like to make boneless roasts from lamb shoulders, but if you want to debone the shoulder and use the meat for sausage, this is the perfect opportunity to do so.

❖ Place the shoulder section in front of you on the lamb's back and saw in half.

❖ Now it is time to debone one of the shoulders. Place the fat side of the shoulder fat side down on the table with the bone side up; now you will proceed to remove the entire rib cage, chine bone (or spine), and breastbone in one shot.

❖ Now that you have released the entire rib cage, keep scraping at the bone to finish releasing the bone from the muscle. **11**

❖ You now have two bones left to remove—the scapula and a small piece of the shank. The scapula and the sawed-off shank meet together like your arm and your shoulder blade. The scapula, or elephant ear, is toward the top portion of this piece. You are essentially making a faith cut at this point. With the fat side down, plunge your knife into the point where the shoulder pivots. You should hit bone, and your knife will go in no farther than about ⅛ inch.

❖ Drag your knife up and down along the middle of the scapula, cleaning the edges of the bone. Continue past the bulb of the joint, pulling muscle away from the shank bone as you go. After you have finished cleaning muscle away from the edges of the bone, pulling back with your fingers as you go, slip the tip of your knife underneath the shank and, with short, quick cuts, pull the bone and scapula out of the shoulder. The shoulder is now ready to be rolled and tied (see page 94 for tying techniques). You can cut the roast in half, or even thirds, after you tie it up. Repeat the steps with other shoulder. You will have two to six beautiful boneless roasts. Save the bones for stock.

The outer surface of all lamb fat is covered by fell, a thin, paperlike covering. It should not be removed from roasts and legs because it helps these cuts retain their shape and juiciness during cooking.

Saddle

The money meat is next—start with the rib section, home to those delectable tiny chops.

RIBS

❖ Place the rib cage fat side down and saw through the spine, following the length of the spine. Finish the cut with your 5-inch knife. **12**

❖ Using your 5-inch knife, scrape fat away from the spine *inside* the rib cage. This should help to reveal the spine and make it easier to cut. Then, using your saw, cut on both sides of the chine bone at a 45-degree angle toward the spine. Take care not to cut into the eyes of the rib chops. Finish the cut with your 5-inch knife. Continuing with your knife, cut down the feather bones (these are the ones connected to the chine) to free the eye muscle without cutting into the meat. The result is a de-chined lamb rack. Repeat on the other side.

❖ The bones are too long at this point, so run your knife across the ribs about 1 inch down from the top, and then snap the tops clean off. Feel for a soft spot that will help guide you to where you should break.

❖ French the ribs following the instructions on page 98. **13**

These racks can be roasted whole or cut into individual chops at this point.

LOIN

❖ Split the loin in half in the same way you split the ribs. Position the bottom of the loin, or tail, toward you. Cut most of the tail off for a lean roast; for a fattier roast, leave the tail on.

❖ Place the fat side down and find the tenderloin. This will be obvious. Use your 5-inch knife to release the tenderloin from the bone. The tenderloin will still be held on to the roast by a thread of muscle; if it falls off, don't worry—you can always tuck it back up into the roast. Flip the loin over so that it is fat side up and cut the length of the loin by placing your 5-inch knife underneath the feather bones, until you hit the spine, then drag your knife all the way across.

❖ Cut across the top of the loin and drag your knife straight down against the bone, releasing the muscle. Slowly peel the muscle away from the bone. Remove the T-bone; roll, wrap, and tie the roast. Cut it in half for two roasts. Repeat on other side.

Always count twice and cut once!

Legs

All that's left for you to break down is the legs.

❖ Split the legs in half the same way you split the loin and ribs. **14**

Removing the Sirloin

This is the time for your 8-inch knife. You want to make this cut with your knife at a 15- to 20-degree angle. To do so, place the bottom of the blade with the part closest to the hilt or handle next to the aitch bone. The tip of the knife should be touching the tailbone. Draw the knife down from the tailbone to the aitch bone toward you, making a very slight incision. You cannot go deeper because you are literally on top of bone. **15** Follow this with your bone saw, cutting right through the bone. **16** Then follow through with your 8-inch knife as you have done in previous steps. Now you have removed the sirloin from the leg. Repeat on the other leg. Roast the sirloin whole, bone-in.

❖ Remove the pelvic bone by cutting along the aitch or hip bone. Cut through the socket of the joint. Remove the femur by cutting along the natural seam of the leg muscle. Cut around the base of the bone to release. Cut around the knee cap and remove. (For a more detailed description of removing the femur and butterflying the leg, see page 123.)

You should have been wrapping (see page 101) and chilling the meat throughout the breakdown, so now is the time to sit down, pop open a beer, and reflect on how much easier the process will be the next time—if you ever decide to do it again!

Now is the time to sit down, pop open a beer.

QUICK LAMB MEATBALLS

Everyone who visits our house on a regular basis has these meatballs at least once. Served with pita, a green salad, Israeli couscous, and a yogurt sauce, this is one of Jessica's go-to meals: quick, cheap, and easy to make. If you have the time, grind your own meat; it's easy when you use a KitchenAid with an attachment. Start with a not-too-lean cut like shoulder (remember, fat is flavor). Cut the meat into small chunks, discarding any hard pieces of fat or sinew. If all you have is a food processor, then process, pulsing the machine on and off a couple of times to get the consistency you need (you may have to run the grind through again if you are using a stand mixer). If you want to get fancy, throw a small onion or garlic in with the meat as you grind it.

❖ **SERVES 4**

---

1 pound ground lamb (shoulder or stew meat)

2 garlic cloves, minced

2 tablespoons chopped fresh cilantro (optional)

2 teaspoons harissa (see Note)

1 teaspoon kosher salt

½ teaspoon freshly ground black pepper

Yogurt Sauce (recipe follows)

Note: *Harissa, a North African spice paste, varies from region to region, so there is no definitive recipe, but a mixture of 1 teaspoon ground cumin, ½ teaspoon ground chile, and 1 teaspoon smoked paprika is a good substitute.*

Preheat the oven to 350°F.

In a large bowl, combine the lamb, garlic, cilantro if using, harissa, salt, and pepper. Roll 1-tablespoon balls between your palms and place on a rimmed baking sheet.

Set a large ovenproof pan over medium heat. When the pan is hot, add the meatballs and sear on all sides, 3 to 5 minutes total. Transfer to the oven and cook the meatballs for 4 to 6 minutes, until the insides are pink and the outsides are golden brown. Transfer to a serving dish, drizzle yogurt sauce over the top, and serve.

YOGURT SAUCE
MAKES ABOUT 1 CUP

1 cup plain yogurt

2 tablespoons chopped fresh cilantro or mint (optional)

1 teaspoon harissa

A squeeze of lemon juice

Salt and freshly ground black pepper

In a medium bowl, combine the yogurt, cilantro if using, harissa, and lemon juice; season with salt and pepper. Whisk until the yogurt is thin and creamy. Keep in the refrigerator for up to 7 days.

GRILLED BUTTERFLIED LEG OF LAMB
WITH AN INDIAN-STYLE WET RUB

Grilling is our favorite way to cook lamb. Lamb lends itself to the grill like no other meat. Perhaps it's because lamb's essential earthiness stands up to the smoke and char, yet its fat protects the meat. Whatever it is, there is nothing better than coming home on a summer night and throwing a butterflied leg of lamb on the grill. Rub it with a little olive oil, salt, pepper, and garlic and you've got a fantastic dinner in 20 minutes—or try this Indian-style rub. Just remember, lamb is a fatty meat, so beware of flare-ups: always watch your meat closely, and move it to the top rack if you feel that it is getting done too fast or runs the risk of burning. ❖ **SERVES 6**

2 teaspoons garam masala

1½ teaspoons ground coriander

1 teaspoon ground cumin

½ teaspoon cayenne

½ teaspoon freshly ground black pepper, plus more for serving

1½ teaspoons coarse salt, plus more for serving

1 teaspoon peeled grated fresh ginger

1 garlic clove, minced

½ teaspoon brown sugar

2 tablespoons olive oil, plus more for the grill

1 (5- to 6-pound) boneless, butterflied leg of lamb, untied (ask your butcher to do this for you or see opposite)

In a small, heavy-bottomed skillet set over medium heat, combine the garam masala, coriander, cumin, cayenne, and black pepper. Toast the spices, stirring frequently and being careful not to burn them, for 2 to 3 minutes, until the spices turn a shade darker. This releases the aromatic oils and improves the flavor of the rub. Remove the pan from the heat immediately and transfer the spices to a glass or metal bowl.

Add the salt, ginger, garlic, and brown sugar to the toasted spices and mix thoroughly. While stirring, slowly add the oil until a thick paste forms.

Score the meat by making small cuts all over the fat side of the lamb. Rub the lamb with the spice paste and place it in a glass or ceramic dish or a plastic bag. Let it sit for 30 minutes at room temperature, or up to 3 hours in the refrigerator. Remove from the refrigerator and let sit for 30 minutes before grilling.

Heat a grill to medium. Lightly oil the grates. Grill the lamb, covered, until an instant-read thermometer inserted in thickest part of the meat registers 120°F for medium-rare, 6 to 8 minutes per side.

Remove the lamb from the grill. Sprinkle it with additional salt and pepper, tent it loosely with aluminum foil, and let it rest for 5 minutes. Thinly slice the lamb and serve.

BUTTERFLYING A LEG OF LAMB

Removing the femur bone from a leg allows the meat to cook quickly and evenly. Buy a 6- to 7-pound leg of lamb from your butcher. Ask him or her to remove the aitchbone, sirloin, and shank. The leg should be well cleaned of fat. See the first color photograph insert for step-by-step instructions.

❖ Place the leg on a cutting board. Holding your 5-inch boning knife in a pistol grip, look for the seam that runs parallel to the bone. Using only the tip of the knife, make one long cut running the length of the femur. Let the bone guide you; you are opening the seam as you go and exposing the bone on one side. Start by cutting into the portion of the leg facing away from you on the table. The knife should be parallel with the bone, scraping up against it. Drag the knife straight through the muscle toward you, scraping the tip alongside the bone the entire time. Let the bone guide you down.

❖ Pull the cut muscle apart with the hand not holding the knife, and run the knife along the opposite side of the bone from the one you just cut. 1

❖ Keep scraping the meat from the bone while pulling the muscle back with your other hand until it is free except for the hinged kneecap or patella. 2

❖ Stand the bone up and run the tip of the knife around the kneecap until it pops free. This takes a bit of wiggling. Do not cut into the flesh.

❖ Lay the deboned leg fat side down and cut out any glands or sinew.

❖ There should be two sections of meat that are thicker than the rest of the leg; these need to be scored using the natural seams with 2 to 3 shallow vertical cuts to flatten or butterfly the meat. 3

❖ Turn the leg over and score the fat side with 5 to 6 shallow cuts. Do not cut into the meat. 4

WARM LAMB SALAD WITH POMEGRANATE

Jessica loves this recipe. She saw Nigella Lawson do something similar on her show a couple of years ago, adapted it, and hasn't stopped making it since. I think she loves that she gets to beat up a pomegranate every time she makes this, but she claims it's a showstopper that makes her look good with almost no effort at all. This is another great use of lamb shoulder (a wildly underutilized cut) and the perfect braising recipe. In fact, we often suggest using a Crock-Pot for this recipe. ❖ **SERVES 6 TO 8**

---

1 (5-pound) boneless lamb shoulder, cleaned and tied (see Note)

4 shallots, unpeeled, halved

6 garlic cloves

Coarse sea salt

2 cups chicken stock (preferably homemade), or half lamb and half chicken stock

2 heads arugula or watercress

Small handful of chopped fresh mint

1 pomegranate

2 tablespoons pomegranate molasses or POM juice (optional)

2 tablespoons pine nuts, toasted (optional)

3 tablespoons crumbled feta cheese (optional)

Pita bread, warmed, for serving

Note: *This recipe can also be made with anything braisable, like shanks or country-style ribs.*

Preheat the oven to 325°F.

Heat a large ovenproof pot over medium heat. Add the lamb and brown it on all sides, 6 to 8 minutes total. Transfer the lamb to a platter. Add the shallots and garlic to the pot and cook, stirring, until they are soft and golden brown, about 4 minutes. Add a pinch of salt to the pot, then pour in the stock and bring the mixture to a boil. Return the lamb to the pot, cover, and transfer to the oven.

Roast the lamb for about 5 hours, until the lamb is literally falling apart. Take the lamb out of the oven and let it cool in the pot.

About an hour before you want to eat, take the lamb out of the pot. Cut and remove the twine. Remove as much of the fat as possible and shred the meat into uniform pieces with two forks.

Put the arugula on a platter and put the shredded lamb on top. Sprinkle with sea salt and the chopped mint. Cut the pomegranate in half. Hold one pomegranate half above the plate and hit the back of it with a wooden spoon to knock out the seeds.

Take the other half of the pomegranate and squeeze its juice over the salad. If you want a juicier, stronger, fruitier salad, add a couple of tablespoons of pomegranate molasses. Scatter the toasted pine nuts and feta cheese over the top, if desired.

Serve the salad while the lamb is still warm (cold lamb fat congeals unappetizingly), with warmed pita on the side.

LAMB SIRLOIN

Lamb sirloin is one of those cuts that is hard to find but worth the effort. It's the bottom of the loin toward the leg and it's delicious. Most butcher shops sell the sirloin as part of the whole leg, and we used to use it for stew meat—both terrible wastes. My employees convinced me to use it for a roast—a great example of the fact that this business is run by a team. It makes a fast, easy roast that is smaller and more tender than a traditional leg. It feeds a family of three like ours perfectly. My favorite way to eat it is in gyros: slice it thin and put it in a pita with a dab of Yogurt Sauce (page 121). Or serve it more elegantly with roasted veggies and Israeli couscous.

❖ **SERVES 2 TO 3**

1 (1½- to 2-pound) lamb sirloin, cleaned
    and tied
2 tablespoons olive oil
2 tablespoons chopped fresh rosemary
1 tablespoon finely grated lemon zest
1 garlic clove, minced
Kosher salt

Preheat the oven to 350°F.

    Place the lamb, fat side up, in a large roasting pan. In a small bowl, combine the oil, rosemary, lemon zest, and garlic to create a paste. Rub the paste all over the lamb, then sprinkle the lamb with salt.

    Roast the lamb, basting occasionally with the pan juices, until an instant-read thermometer inserted into the thickest part of the meat registers 120°F for medium-rare, about 50 minutes.

    Transfer the lamb to a platter, tent it loosely with aluminum foil, and let it rest for 10 minutes. Cut and remove the twine. Cut the lamb into thin slices and arrange the slices on a platter. Pour the pan juices over the meat and serve.

PORK IS THE SEXIEST OF ALL MEATS. There's just something about it. Perhaps it's the delicious, voluptuous fat or the way the skin crisps to a crackling crunch that seems to satisfy the most carnal of urges. Whatever it is, it sends our friends and customers alike into paroxysms of pleasure. Pork is a meat so purely sensual that it has become a verb. No matter the cut, if you ask people what really rocks their world, the answer is always the pig. Chicharrones, cheeks, and pig tails—from nose to belly to butt, the pig never fails to elicit some sort of almost chemical reaction. We have participated in many events based entirely on a pig-themed menu— the lowly chicken never gets that kind of honor, nor does the pastoral lamb. And it's the pig that brings on the hoarse whisper over the counter, "Yeah, just throw in a couple of those chops, yeah, the *thick* ones . . . ," or the furtive look accompanied by "Have you got any lard? I was thinking of frying some potatoes."

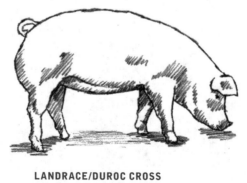

LANDRACE/DUROC CROSS

Jess and I have talked about this link between pork and pleasure endlessly. She is a confirmed lamb lover, so as much as she adores pork, the fact that lamb is underappreciated is a crime in her book. She says loving lamb is part of our Semitic heritage, but I disagree. I think that is why I love pork all the more; to Jews as well as Muslims, it's the forbidden fruit, a truly divisive protein. In fact, to this day when my father comes to dinner we can't serve pork. We tried once (we made a ham for Passover, oy!), but it didn't go over very well. But it's so good that many people make exceptions to the no-pork-eating rule. My dad's is bacon. This goes for everyone else we know, too.

Ah, bacon. If there is a crack cocaine cut of meat, this is it. If bacon doesn't lead you into the nether regions of the meat-eating world, nothing will. Ours is salt-packed, rubbed with pepper, basted with apple cider, and then hot-smoked—no nitrates, no nitrites. It has a cult following. Sitting in the case it looks ostentatiously fatty. This abundance of fat renders perfectly, and the result is melt-in-your-mouth satisfaction. It helps that the bellies we smoke come from local pastured pigs that thrive on a steady diet of goodness. Not surprisingly, it has converted more than a few vegetarians and vegans.

Our bacon was the first meat I sunk my teeth into after almost two decades as a vegan. I browned a knuckle-deep-thick slab—bacon cutlets, really—on each side and ate big hunks of it as soon as I could. Standing not sitting. Straight from the pan into my mouth. They were almost raw and unreal—crispy outside and explosive-creamy inside. It has a salty, smoky, very lightly sweet flavor that you just don't get from seitan. I must have eaten three whole pigs' worth of bellies within a couple of weeks. Not everyone morphs into a complete carnivore like I did. We know vegetarians who indulge in bacon. We won't point fingers—we're always happy to supply their fix—and we are certainly not here to judge, but come on, people, bacon is *not* a vegetable.

Depending on the time of year and customer demand, our pigs come from three to five nearby family farms that we've sussed out, tasted through, like, and trust. The animals are being raised outside and are eating local corn, veggies, and apples, as well as forage. Our farmers do their own breeding. Pigs—who should spend eight to ten hours a day rooting, exploring, and generally creating chaos wherever they go—are smart animals whose intelligence equals that of a dog. We would never keep a dog in a crate all day with nothing to chew on or to play with. So it's important to us that our pigs are wandering around in big outdoor pens and rotated to other pens and pasture once they've destroyed everything in their wake, as they always do.

BREEDS

When we first opened Fleisher's, we were all about the popular heritage breeds—Ossabows, Berkshires, Tamworths—and that's what we sold. But over time we kept running into genetic and breeding-related issues with them, so we turned to our farmers—who know more about these things than we do, go figure—and decided to give up the marketing game and return to the classics. We now sell white and black Landrace/Duroc crosses, which are sturdy enough to go up against winter in the Northeast. Landrace are good mothers who birth large litters, and Durocs are an extremely hardy older breed that produces quality meat. In this case the old adage proved right: mutts truly are healthier than purebreds. They also taste great—they're as full-flavored as any of the heritage breeds. It's the good breeding plus all that moving around that intensifies the flavor. And, of course, the meat is much darker than supermarket pork from pigs bred and raised to be what the National Pork Board famously dubbed "the other white meat." To the untrained eye, some of our cuts may even look like something other than pig—lamb or veal. The fat cap (that layer of fat between the spine and the top of the skin) and intramuscular fat are fantastic—and there's much more of it than in a conventionally raised animal that has all of the fat bred out of it, but not as much as in heritage breeds like the fatty Ossabow, which are literally raised for fat. This balance is good for us; butchers lose money on fat, and make it on muscle.

That said, you might come to the store one day and find a heritage roast. We don't discriminate! The range of what a sustainable butcher sells always has to do with what's available and what's seasonal.

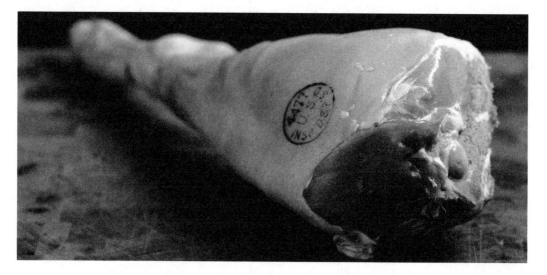

PEDIGREE PIGS

These days the most talked about pigs are the ones with pedigrees. That's because most chefs, restaurateurs, farmers, and even knowledgeable consumers are trying to get away from the skinny swine that began to populate the food landscape in the 1970s. Before then, back in the good old days, pigs—and their fat—were so important that they were divided into those who produced great bacon and those who produced great lard. At one time, pig fat was even considered more valuable than meat because of its crucial role in cooking, candle making, and soap production. Thankfully in recent years some farmers have begun to realize that reducing fat and compromising flavor isn't a good thing, that fat *adds* flavor, and that the leanest possible pig may not be a goal to strive for. Though we don't usually sell pedigrees, there are so many heritage breeds around that we thought we should give you an idea of what you might find out there in hog heaven.

BERKSHIRE This pork, also known as Kurobuta, is prized among the Japanese, who favor a fatty pig. We like to think of them as the Wagyu of the pig world. (That's the Japanese breed of beef known for its abundance of intramuscular fat.)

GLOUCESTERSHIRE OLD SPOT Hands down this breed has the cutest piglets—guaranteed to make a grown man (even a butcher . . .) fall to his knees. Their high fat-to-meat ratio makes them great baconaters.

OSSABOW A cousin to the Iberian black pig known throughout the world for the Ibérico *jamón* (ham) it produces, the Ossabow was brought to this country by the Spanish explorers who could not conceive of traveling to the New World without bringing their own lunch. It's known for a thick, golden, soft fat cap that melts like *buttah*.

TAMWORTH These vaguely scholarly-looking animals with close-set eyes and tufts of reddish bed-head hair have a reputation for producing superb bacon.

PASTURED VS. ORGANIC VS. CONVENTIONAL

Conventional supermarket pork comes from animals that have never lived or breathed outside a sterile factory farm, never stepped a hoof on the earth, never rooted in the dirt. Animals that have been bred to live exclusively in confinement are so scrawny that they would freeze outside anyway. They're also so delicate that people entering their confinement operation have to wear masks and shoe covers so the animals don't get sick(er). To prevent disease outbreaks and to stimulate faster growth, the commercial hog industry is said to add more than 10 million pounds of antibiotics to its feed yearly, which is, by some accounts, up to eight times more than all the antibiotics used to treat human illnesses in that same time frame.

In addition to the antibiotics, confinement pigs are fed cheap crap. So it should come as no surprise that their meat tastes like it. Even if you do the research and know something about how your ham was raised and treated, you won't see what a butcher sees. We see, for instance, that pastured pigs have clean glands—they're almost the same color as the flesh. Glands are the filters for the body, and they reflect what the animals have been through. On our pigs, they are pearlescent and clear. On a conventionally raised pig, those glands are brown to black. One of our colleagues told us this before we saw

---

FUN THINGS TO DO WITH PORK FAT

❖ Make candles

❖ Turn it into soap

❖ Render it for lard (see page 67), then make wonderfully flaky piecrusts

❖ Fry potatoes in it

❖ Make chicharrones (aka fried pork rinds, made from copious amounts of fat with the skin attached)

❖ Try making salt pork

❖ Fry chicken in it (see page 212)

---

it, and we didn't believe him. Then one time while I was learning to make charcuterie at someone else's shop, I ran into a gray/black gland. It was disgusting. Often these glands are not removed before the meat is ground or processed.

If well-raised and -fed pastured pork isn't available near you, USDA organic is absolutely a far safer, better bet than conventional. Always read labels and ask questions; just because something is certified organic doesn't mean it's local or that it has roamed free.

AFTER SLAUGHTER

During the winter we do about seven or eight pigs a week. In the summer, when life is all about barbecue, this number can jump to twelve. It also jumps around Christmas. The hogs are big—somewhere between 180 and 250 pounds, and about seven to nine months old. Their age depends on several factors: how fast they are growing; how many we need; how pissed off they are (angry pigs can maim each other—i.e., harm our product—so these are often killed younger); the time of year (pigs are angrier in summer months—you would be, too, if you were 200 pounds and hugging a pine tree for shade). Conventional pigs, on the other hand, tend to be slaughtered around five or six months. Pastured animals always take longer to gain weight because they're working off their varied diet as they roam around.

We bring the pigs into the shop in halves, feet and tails on, heads off. We like to let them hang in our cooler—unwrapped—for a week. This concentrates the flavor and makes them easier to cut. Commercial pork gets wrapped in plastic and is slippery. When our pigs come in, their skin feels a little tougher than human skin, but basically the texture is identical. After they sit for a week it's much tougher—dry, nice and firm. Then we cut them up.

Touching the skin of a hanging pig never fails to remind us how similar we

BY ANY OTHER NAME

BARROW A castrato—a snipped male

BOAR The sperm bank—an uncastrated breeder; the pheromones they give off are referred to as "boar taint"

GILT A female who has yet to have piglets

HOG Bigger than 100 pounds

PIG Unlike *cows,* this term can be used for all swine—male, female, old and young (though you do run into some farmers who use *pig* only for youngsters and *hog* for old guys)

SOW A female who has already had piglets

are to what we eat. Humans are animals, so of course we share the same organs, the same senses, the same basic needs. This is what makes many of us want to be vegans or ethical eaters. Pigs drive this sentiment home more than the other animals we sell. When we started Fleisher's we used to get what we called Parson's Pigs, after the farmer. He was growing them for medical use—valve transplants and the like; pigs and humans are that anatomically close. Because they were going into the human body, they had to be pristine—no juice, pure feed, just good clean living. These pigs were worth tens of thousands of dollars but only if they were absolutely perfect. If there was so much as a toenail dinged or a tail nipped, Parson sold them to us. It says a lot about our society that pigs supplying transplant parts have to be perfect and well raised and well fed, but those raised for conventional meat we Americans swallow are sick and eat crap. We've heard of a place in San Francisco that sells a similar thing—the beef from animals harvested for the fat that plastic surgeons use for collagen injections.

AGE MATTERS

We don't do many sucklings for a bunch of reasons. For farmers, they're expensive to raise and not cost-effective to sell; more money is always made on a full-grown animal. Tastewise, there's no finish to suckling, no earthy depth. And then there's the guilt. Despite what we say about veal (see page 179), butchers do have limits. We don't do bears (their muscle structure is too close to a human's) and we try not to do baby pigs. When one of our farmers has enough going and can manage it, we'll do some small-ish pigs, teenagers really—about 35 pounds versus 14 pounds for a true two- to six-week-old suckling. As soon as they start hanging out at the 7-Eleven, smoking cigarettes, and asking

people to buy them beer, we knock them down. Pigs this size are good for porchetta, which we train our apprentices to make as part of their program. And some of our customers want them because the presentation—little pig with head and feet—is phenomenal. So we suggest them, plus shoulders or legs, as alternatives to people who order sucklings.

DON'T OVERDO IT

For years the general rule for pork was to cook it until it was dry, leathery, and white; however, we suggest that you eat your pork at a juicy medium-rare. Overcooking was born out of a fear of trichinosis, a justifiable but somewhat outdated concern. We aren't saying that the parasites that cause the disease don't exist, but incidences in the United States from pork are rare, and are more likely to come from undercooked wild game (even then, the numbers are low). According to the Centers for Disease Control, an average of twelve cases per year were reported from 1997 to 2001. This is clearly no reason to do something as tragic as ruining good pork by overcooking it.

PRIMAL PRIMER

When you stand in front of our cases, you may see cuts you don't see in a supermarket because they don't come in a box, like a country-style rib or a sirloin roast off the end of the loin. And you always see more fat. It protects the meat from overcooking and of course adds flavor. When we first began butchering, we used to leave a ½-inch fat cap on all our chops but customers complained, so now we trim as much as we can bear to.

Most of the pigs we buy are about 225 pounds, and we are able to use 95 percent of the animal (those efficient little buggers!). The four primals we choose to break from a pig are the shoulder (aka the butt, said to be named after the bar-rels they were stored in around the time of the Revolutionary War, not, as most people think, after the behind of the swine), the loin, the belly, and the leg (aka the ham). These primals basically divide the pig into three sections: front (sausage), middle (two sections of money meat—chops or loin and bacon), and rear (hams or roasts). Our way of cutting up a pig is different from what others butchers do.

The *shoulder*, which weighs about 25 pounds, is known for braising and sausage meat and is commonly broken into two main subprimals, the picnic (lower shoulder) and the butt (upper shoulder). Confusingly, the butt is often called the Boston butt (everywhere in the country

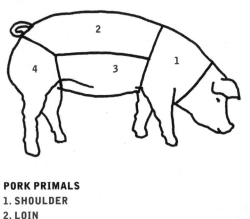

PORK PRIMALS
1. SHOULDER
2. LOIN
3. BELLY
4. LEG

PORK SUBPRIMALS
1. TOP ROUND
2. SHANK
3. HAM
4. SIRLOIN TOP
5. CENTER CUT LOIN
6. RIB LOIN
7. BUTT
8. PICNIC HAM
9. CHEEK
10. JOWL
11. BELLY
12. SPARE RIBS
13. BABY BACK RIBS

except Boston!) or the shoulder butt. To further confuse you, the picnic can also be referred to as the picnic ham or the picnic shoulder. We like our butts long because we believe tougher shoulder chops, which we make into country-style ribs, should not be confused with tender loin chops. We do this by cutting our shoulders off right between the fifth and sixth ribs. Most commercial processors cut behind the first rib to get a longer loin.

The *loin* with the fatback attached can weigh upwards of 25 pounds and is filled with the cuts that people love to roast or grill, like chops, roasts, and baby back ribs. The loin extends from the sixth rib to the fourteenth (pigs have fourteen ribs per side, unlike other animals) and contains the tenderest muscle.

The *belly*, which falls below the loin, is about 15 pounds of fatty goodness and provides bacon, lard, and spareribs. The belly should be fatty but firm—soft, mushy bellies are found on only the very young or the very old.

The *leg* (aka the ham) weighs about 30 pounds and creates all those delicious hams that the Deep South, Italy, and Spain are known for. This region of muscles is extremely well worked, so curing or smoking makes this tougher primal tender.

Cook This Way

SHOULDER You can roast, braise, or smoke any of these very versatile cuts.

    Boston butt—roast or braise or smoke

    Foot/trotter—pickle or braise

    Hock—smoke or braise and/or deep-fry

    Picnic ham—braise or roast or grind for sausage

LOIN The loin is filled with things people love to roast, grill, and smoke—the most tender and costly cuts of pork.

    Baby back ribs—smoke or grill or bake

    Back fat—cure to make lardo

    Bone-in or bone-out chops (aka center-cut chops)—stovetop to oven (see page 90) or grill, or brine and smoke

    Leaf lard—use to bake or fry

    Loin roast—roast or cure to make Canadian bacon

Tenderloin—roast or stir-fry

Top sirloin—roast

BELLY All that is good is found here; the cuts lend themselves almost totally to smoking but can be braised and roasted as well.

    Belly—braise or fry or cure or smoke for bacon

    Ribs—smoke or grill or bake (low and slow for all three)

LEG Some of the least expensive cuts on a pig can be literally turned into gold: think prosciutto, Serrano ham, and *jamón ibérico*.

    Ham—smoke or roast

    Hock—braise or smoke or deep-fry

    Top round—turn into pork cutlets and pan-sear

    Trotter—pickle or braise

    Whole leg—cure (prosciutto or Serrano ham)

 SEAR/ROAST/STOVETOP TO OVEN

GRIND/SAUSAGE

BRAISE/SMOKE

ROAST

VARIETY MEATS

Ears—roast or braise

Head—use for headcheese or pull cheeks for braise

Jowls—cure (guanciale)

Skin—fry to make chicharrones, or pork rinds

Tail—braise

CHARCUTERIE

We don't do much charcuterie at the shop: we specialize in fresh meat, not cured or processed products. In France, the charcutier and the butcher work in two different shops. It's not the same gig. Still, because we work with whole animals, we are able to do some bacon, ham, sausage, bresaola, and guanciale. We try to keep it simple, so I have a nothing-can-be-aged-more-than-thirty-days rule that limits what I make. My rule is partly economic and partly a space consideration; a ham hanging for a year earns no income and

NOSE TO TAIL

We use all animal parts and scraps (trim) but it's the rare customer who truly wants to eat the actual nose or tail, despite an ever-growing fondness for that catchphrase. So we have pig heads. Some go to wholesale. I do some guanciale for the shop—dry cured pork jowls hung for thirty days—but mainly I keep the cheeks; they're my favorite pieces of pork in the world. No one seems to want the pig tails, though. It's a shame because they are succulent little digit-sized morsels of skin and fat. Braise them first—the fat just melts away—then crisp them in your oven. They're like an edgier chicken wing.

THE BEST PORK CHEEKS EVER

If you happen to have a pig head, remove the cheeks, or buy them from your butcher. If they aren't already cleaned, take off the sinew and fat. Put the cheeks in a saucepan with enough stock (chicken or pork) to almost cover them, then braise them for an hour and a half. They should be tender but not falling apart. Pat them dry and chill them until they are cool to the touch. Dredge the cheeks first in a beaten egg, then panko bread crumbs seasoned with salt and freshly ground pepper; do it again then deep-fry them in lard. You're welcome.

ties up valuable real estate. I actually love making charcuterie, and it's easy to try at home (see page 143). The first thing you will need is a cool, dark, and somewhat humid (50 to 60 percent humidity) space. A cellar works well. The next is great meat. You are showcasing the meat—usually adding nothing more to it than salt—so it has to be the best-tasting product you can find. The third thing you'll need is time. My thirty-day rule doesn't apply to you, so age your hams for as long as you like.

SALT

I love salt so much that Jessica sometimes jokes about installing a salt lick next to my side of the bed. Salt plays a very important role in a butcher's daily life. We salt our boards at the end of the day to sterilize them, we salt our hams and eye rounds to cure them, and we always salt our cooked meat to bring out flavor. It's incredible that salt can do so much: kill bacteria, preserve meat and vegetables, and make everything it touches taste better.

At the shop we use a lot of sea salt—both fine and coarse grind. Its trace minerals add a particularly important flavor when curing meat. Yet each kind of salt—its salinity, its crystal size—is different. This makes it difficult to recommend amounts in recipes or to interchange salts. We use a lot of kosher salt as well. It's the same as regular old table salt but with bigger, flaky crystals that adhere well to meat. As far as brands go, at home we use Diamond (Jessica grew up with it), and at the shop we use Morton's, which has bigger crystals and therefore less punch (which means I am always oversalting at home). A more accurate measurement of salt other than sticking with the same brand is weight.

Aside from sea salt and kosher salt, our cabinets are loaded with fancy salts that look pretty—pink, gray, and even black—and taste even better. Maldon, which has a light, crisp crunch and comes in pyramid-shaped flakes, is a favorite finishing salt to use at the end of a recipe. Whether the ingredient is meat, salt, or pepper: choose the best one and your meal, however simple, will be spectacular.

Salt plays a very important role in a butcher's daily life.

NITRITES

We may have Peruvian pink salt on our shelves at home, but when butchers talk about pink, or curing, salt they are referring to nitrites. Ordinary table salt is sodium chloride; curing salt is sodium chloride with nitrites added to it. It is colored pink to keep it from getting mixed up with regular salt, since this stuff in large amounts can be dangerous. Nitrites do three really important things to meat: they retain that great, almost cartoony pink or red color (think about a commercially produced ham), they prevent the fat from going rancid, and they keep bacteria that cause botulism from growing in the meat. All are especially important in cured meat products that are cold-smoked or air-dried and then not cooked. Cold smoking can be particularly dangerous: the temperatures used hover around only 100°F, which doesn't cook the meat at all but rather opens its pores, allowing the smoke to penetrate and create a smoky flavor. It also provides a perfect breeding ground for bacteria. This is why the federal government demands that commercial producers of charcuterie use nitrites in their products.

Unfortunately nitrites have been linked to cancer in various studies, specifically colon cancer and childhood leukemia. You might have heard the same about nitrates, which basically convert to nitrites. When meats containing nitrites are exposed to high temperatures they form carcinogenic nitrosamines.

Natural and organic meat processors rely on things like spinach and celery juice because they contain natural nitrites (which are, by the way, chemically identical to synthetic nitrates). The only nitrates we use for our products—such as hot dogs, ham, bacon, and hocks—are the naturally occurring ones found in sea salt. And we hot-smoke—essentially cook—our hams, bacon, and chops. And we cure the products that are *not* heated, like bresaola and coppa (dry cured pork from the neck/shoulder section) with sea salt.

Home Fabrication

Because they're smaller than steer, and because people really, really love pork, pigs are what people who want to carve and cure at home tend to start with. If you haven't read *Heat* author Bill Buford's epic *New Yorker* article about sourcing, then wrangling a whole pig back to his New York City apartment, complete with Vespa and elevator scenes, do so now. If you're interested in attempting this folly, we don't suggest asking for a whole pig, since the entire carcass doesn't fit in the average fridge. Instead, see if you can locate a pork leg. Once you get your hands on one, you'll want to make prosciutto.

PROSCIUTTO

In Heat, *Buford describes talking to an old Italian butcher, who says, "When I was young, there was one kind of prosciutto. It was made in the winter, by hand, and aged for two years. It was sweet when you smelled it. A profound perfume. Unmistakable. To age a prosciutto is a subtle business. If it's too warm, the aging process never begins. The meat spoils. If it's too dry, the meat is ruined. It needs to be damp but cool. The summer is too hot. In the winter—that's when you make salumi. Your prosciutto. Your soppressata. Your sausages."*

When you think of prosciutto, making it at home might not be the first thing that comes to mind. But it's possible.

Tell your butcher or farmer what you're up to and ask for one pork leg, skin on, preferably from an older pig with a decent fat cap on it. It should weigh 15 to 20 pounds, but that varies from pig to pig. It will lose about 50 percent of its weight after it cures. Ask for the sirloin and aitchbone removed. You want it hock on (including the gambrel, or Achilles tendon), clean, and hairless. It should be dried for a week in the cooler (have your butcher do this for you), free of mold, dry and stiff to the touch. There should be no smell. ❖ **MAKES A 7- TO 12-POUND PROSCIUTTO**

---

25 pounds coarse sea salt

1 ounce InstaCure #2, DQ Curing Salt #2, or other long-term curing salt (optional; see discussion on page 141 and Note)

2 cups juniper berries, coarsely cracked (optional)

2 cups whole black peppercorns, coarsely cracked (optional)

1 (15- to 20-pound) pig leg

EQUIPMENT

Large, very clean, nonreactive tub that can hold 25 pounds of coarse sea salt and the pig leg

Butcher's twine

Cheesecloth

Note: *Our friend Tom Mylan, onetime apprentice and now butcher, convinced us that this prosciutto can even be done in a New York City apartment. He likes to take a few good whacks at the leg with a bat before he starts the curing process (don't go crazy, this is not a Mafia hit) because the blows both tenderize the meat and move blood out of the muscle. Do not hit the bone, which will cause bruising—something you don't want in your ham. He then uses the bat as a rolling pin to press any remaining blood out of the muscle. Because Tom, crazy man that he is, did this in his loft and not a butcher shop with lots of huge coolers, his decisions on how to cure his ham had to be different from ours. Instead of trying to figure out how to fit a pig leg, 25 pounds of salt, and the box that contains it all in an apartment-sized fridge, he used nitrites, or pink salt (see page 141), to circumvent the chilling process. If you are do-*

ing this during the winter and have a nice cold space, like your garage or an enormous extra refrigerator (you lucky dog!), try our method. If you, like Tom, don't have the space to chill, we recommend his method. If you're using pink salt, first mix it into all the salt, then follow the rest of the steps.

Mix 4 cups of the salt with the juniper berries and pepper if using and rub the mixture all over the leg. Bury it completely in a container filled with the remaining salt; place in the refrigerator.

Refrigerate for 28 days (if using pink salt, just keep in a cool space).

Take the leg out of the container and wash it with cool water to remove all the salt. If it doesn't fit in your kitchen sink, use the bathtub (as long as the tub isn't filled with hair and soap scum—clean is crucial). Put the rinsed leg in a non-reactive tub filled with cold water in the refrigerator, and let it soak for 36 hours (if using pink salt, the tub doesn't need to be chilled).

Remove the leg from the tub and dry it well with paper towels.

Wrap the foot in twine and hang it at room temperature or lower (64°F to 68°F; slight fluctuations create character in the ham) for 9 months. Ideally you want to do this in a cool, well-ventilated, relatively humid place, like a basement.

In warmer months, cover the leg with cheesecloth. If you see flies, move the ham somewhere else. But generally leave it alone. Patience is a virtue.

After 9 months it's ready, though barely—many prosciutto makers age their prosciutto for 15 months or more. It's like wine. Cut into it if you must, or let it go longer. To cut, wipe it clean and trim ¼ to ½ inch of the rind away. Do not cut all the rind away unless you are planning on eating the whole thing in one sitting.

To slice the prosciutto, you will need a long, sharp knife; the traditional prosciutto knife is about 1 foot long and ½ inch wide. You can hold the prosciutto while slicing it, or even leave it hanging, but the easiest method is to set it up in a prosciutto holder, which is a large clamp device that lets you stand the prosciutto on edge, with the bone horizontal to the table (you generally begin with the half with the most meat facing up). You can find this equipment online. Slice the prosciutto parallel to the bone, trimming away more rind as necessary. With practice you'll be able to cut thin, even slices. Once you reach the bone, flip the prosciutto over and begin slicing the other side. Once you have trimmed away all the meat, use the prosciutto bone for soup.

Once you cut into the prosciutto, you can keep it at room temperature, but it must be used within 1 month. If the prosciutto starts to smell bad or taste bad, it is bad. Some white mold is okay, but green, black, or blue mold is not. If you see any bad mold, throw it out.

THE BUTCHER SUGGESTS: **PORK CUTLETS**

Veal cutlets bring to mind old-world Italian restaurants and oversauced pasta, while chicken cutlets smack of healthy salads and tasteless hoagies. But the underappreciated pork cutlet—now that's where it's at. We portion them off the top of top rounds—part of the ham, or rump, a sweet spot. Jessica likes to cut them up and stir-fry them with any veggies she has in the house for a quick-fix supper, or sauté them and toss with some soy, ginger, and sesame oil on top of soba noodles. I like to dip them in flour, give them a shake, throw them in a pan with butter, a little sage, and lemon. Good meat doesn't need anything fancy to make it special; it just needs a little fat and a little fire.

SAUSAGE

Sausages are one of the most popular things that we sell at the shop. We have nearly as many different types as there are cuisines in the world and we are always adding more. Sausage making is probably the most fun a butcher can have without taking his knife out (betcha thought I was going to say something different) because you are creating flavor profiles, very often ones that really strike a chord with someone. Brats bring to mind ball games, hot dogs are pure backyard barbecues, and maple breakfast sausage makes you want to stay in bed with the paper.

As the last step in their apprenticeship, our students create a sausage. It's not easy, but we've had some great ones (and some utter failures). Usually we find that apprentices are too meek with their spicing. Sausages demand big, bold flavors and even if you are creating something as simple as an Irish banger or a Polish kielbasa you want those spices to jump out at you. We always use organic spices, ground right before we use them. Then we let the spices sit on the meat in the cooler for 24 hours before we grind it. Making your own sausages is always worth the effort as there are no additives, no fillers, no preservatives or other ingredients that you wouldn't want to eat. We always use natural casings on our sausages. If stuffing is too much work for you, there's nothing wrong with forming your sausage grind into patties instead. Uncased grind is also great for stews, soups, sauces, and things like tacos or tamales.

When it comes to grinding for sausages, we recommend using a meat grinder—either a KitchenAid with a grinder attachment that allows for coarse, medium, or fine grinds or a hand version. We like coarse for our sausages, but some sausages like weisswurst (a German veal and pork sausage) demand a fine grind. Keep in mind that hand grinders aren't the easiest things to use, especially if you're making a lot of sausage.

We favor pork shoulder for our sausage; it's fatty, tasty, and inexpensive. You can use whatever part of the pig, lamb, beef, or chicken that you like, but you want fattier cuts. If you choose a lean meat like chicken, add additional pork fat (or lamb fat like we do), and/or use the fattier chicken thighs. Most butchers are happy to give you a little additional fat for free.

One of the most important aspects of sausage making is proper sanitation and handling. Grinds are much more perishable than whole muscle. Keep your meat chilled until just before you grind it, place your grinder parts in the freezer so that they remain chilled as the meat passes over them, and never make sausage in hot weather.

The following recipes are for two of our most popular sausages—they're classics—not gussied up with anything but pure spices, fresh herbs, and great pork.

SWEET ITALIAN
MAKES 3 POUNDS

3 pounds pork stew meat or boneless
   shoulder, cleaned and cut into ½-inch
   pieces or strips
3 tablespoons whole white peppercorns
2 tablespoons whole black peppercorns
2 tablespoons fennel seeds
2 tablespoons dried sage
2 tablespoons kosher salt
¼ cup garlic powder
2 tablespoons onion powder
½ bunch fresh parsley
¼ hank of natural hog casings (optional;
   you need only about 2 feet of hog
   casings for each pound of sausage
   mixture; see page 150)

As you cut up your meat make sure to
remove any gristle or hard bits of fat; you
don't want any nasty surprises in your
sausage. Make sure that the meat pieces
fit easily into the mouth of the grinder.

In a spice or coffee grinder, grind the
white and black peppercorns, fennel
seeds, sage, and salt to a medium-fine
grind, working in batches if necessary.
Transfer the spices to a large bowl, add
the garlic powder and onion powder, and
mix well. Add the meat and mix until
thoroughly blended with the spices.
Transfer the pork to the refrigerator and
chill (or "sweat") for 24 hours.

Remove the pork mixture from the
refrigerator. Add the parsley and mix
until well blended. To test the flavor,
grind a small amount of the meat, cook
a little patty, and taste. Adjust the spices
accordingly. When you have the flavor
you want, grind the whole mixture into
a chilled metal bowl. The grind should
look like nice fat worms. If the worms
look mushy or are not separating properly it means the grinder blade is not
making good contact with the plate or
the grinder blade is dull. Try reattaching
the plate after thoroughly cleaning the
grinder mechanisms. If this doesn't work,
you may have to buy a new blade.

Stuff the pork into the casings if using
and link (see page 149), or leave the
meat uncased and form it into patties.
Sausages will keep refrigerated for 4 to
5 days and in the freezer for 6 months. If
freezing patties, place sheets of plastic in
between them so they don't stick to each
other.

COOKING YOUR SAUSAGE
Roast them in the oven at 325°F for
15 minutes. Jessica likes to poach
them for about 5 minutes in simmering
water, drain, and then roast them until
crispy on the outside. Either method is
fine; just don't heat your sausages too
fast or they will split.

CHORIZO
MAKES 3 POUNDS

3 pounds pork stew meat or boneless
shoulder, cleaned and cut into ½-inch
pieces or strips
3 tablespoons whole black peppercorns
¼ cup cumin seeds
¼ cup dried oregano
3 tablespoons kosher salt
⅓ cup dried cilantro
⅓ cup garlic powder
¼ cup onion powder
3 tablespoons paprika
¼ cup apple cider vinegar
¼ hank of natural hog casings (optional;
you need only about 2 feet of hog
casings for each pound of sausage
mixture; see opposite)

As you cut up your meat make sure to
remove any gristle or hard bits of fat; you
don't want any nasty surprises in your
sausage. Make sure that the meat pieces
fit easily into the mouth of the grinder.

In a spice or coffee grinder, grind the
peppercorns, cumin, oregano, and salt to
a medium-fine grind, working in batches
if necessary. Transfer the spices to a large
bowl, add the cilantro, garlic powder,
onion powder, paprika, and vinegar and
mix well. Add the meat and mix until
thoroughly blended with the spices. Transfer the pork to the refrigerator and chill
(or let the meat "sweat") for 24 hours.

Remove the pork mixture from the
refrigerator. To test the flavor, grind a
small amount of the meat, cook a little
patty, and taste. Adjust the spices accordingly. When you have the flavor you want,
grind the whole mixture into a chilled
metal bowl. The grind should look like
nice fat worms. If the worms look mushy
or are not separating properly it means
the grinder blade is not making good
contact with the plate or the grinder
blade is dull. Try reattaching the plate
after thoroughly cleaning the grinder
mechanisms. If this doesn't work, you
may have to buy a new blade.

Stuff the pork into the casings if using
and link (see opposite), or leave the
meat uncased and form it into patties.
Sausages will keep for 4 to 5 days in
the refrigerator and in the freezer for
6 months. If freezing patties, place sheets
of plastic in between them so they don't
stick to each other.

The grind should look like nice fat worms.

HOW TO STUFF A SAUSAGE

Stuffing sausage is a task best suited for two people. Make sure you have casings, a grinder, a hand stuffer, and a sausage-stuffing funnel ready and chilled. If you only have a KitchenAid with a grinder/stuffer attachment, make sure *all* the components are well chilled.

❖ Soak the casings in cold water for about 30 minutes.

❖ Grind your meat through a hand grinder or stand mixer and let chill while following the rest of the steps.

❖ Hold one end of the casings to the faucet and rinse the inside thoroughly with cold water (kind of like filling a water balloon).

❖ Secure a sausage-stuffing funnel to a 3-pound hand stuffer. (We prefer hand stuffers because they don't heat up as mixers do.)

❖ Ease one end of the casings onto the funnel, then gather the entire casing on, bunching it together so that it is flush with the funnel's top.

❖ Tie a knot about 1 inch from the end of the casing. Remove the ground pork mixture from the refrigerator and gently put it into the mouth of the stuffer or mixer, making sure the tray is also completely full. One person presses the mixture down through the stuffer tube, using a wood or plastic stomper, while the other person holds the end of the casings onto the grinder cone/funnel with one hand and gently holds the now-cased sausage with the other hand.

❖ When the casing is almost full, detach it from the funnel and tie a knot in the end.

❖ Coil the sausages like a snake and prick the sausages all over with a pin to release excess air.

❖ Twist a 5-inch section in one direction to form a link, take the next 5-inch section and twist in the opposite direction. Keep twisting sections in alternate directions to keep the links from unwinding.

CASING CONUNDRUM

When we first opened Fleisher's, we drove ourselves nuts trying to find organic sausage casings. Even certified organic farmers laughed at us. Casings are intestines. The animals are slaughtered and eviscerated, then the intestines must be turned inside out, scraped, washed out forever, dried out, salted down, and put in packaging. For whatever reason, casings aren't available from organic animals. This is so widely accepted that they're even on the USDA organic exemption list, which means the organic sausage at your supermarket doesn't come in an organic casing. And neither does ours. Our slaughterhouse guys cannot legally give them to us from our own animals, and even if they could,

the process is prohibitively expensive. Our casing options were therefore synthetic (that's right: if you're eating a hot dog or a sausage, it might have been made in plastic, then peeled off), collagen, or "natural." We went for natural.

If you're someone who doesn't eat pork or eats only chicken, you should know that our casings for all of our sausages are either lamb or pork. They come in packages of hanks (or bundles) and they look like used condoms. (No surprise here; you can buy lambskin condoms.) The cost is about $30 for enough to make 300 pounds of sausage. It's okay to make that commitment because sausage casings can last for years refrigerated. Sometimes people want uncased sausage, which just means the casing gets peeled off after the sausage is made. Here's a little sausage trivia: small breakfast sausages are usually made with small lamb casings, and larger sausages like salami might even be steer or cow bung casings that are usually peeled off. You read that right; it is what it sounds like. If you want to make sausages but don't have the stomach for casings at home, make patties instead.

BONE-IN BELLY = SPARERIBS AND BACON

When we do demos, we like to show how easy it is to take one cut and make it into two wildly divergent things. Bone-in belly is the perfect example, and our demo trick can easily be done at home. Many of our customers don't realize that bacon is belly; hence the thick bands of fat and thinner stripes of meat. Our pigs are bred to be fatty and succulent, not waifish—a look that's really prized only in the fashion industry. Nestled against the pig's ample belly are the ribs—these are the spareribs, not baby backs, which are cut from the loin area. When and if we have baby backs in the case—and we usually don't—it means that we're also selling boneless pork chops. We love to nibble on the bone of our chops and assume our customers do as well, so we rarely take the ribs off the loin. Removing the ribs from the belly, on the other hand, leaves you with two of our favorite things: belly for bacon and spareribs. See the first color photograph insert for how it's done.

You should be able to get a bone-in belly from a good butcher shop or farmer. When you get your hands on one, just slide your 5-inch knife right under the bones to pull the ribs off the bacon. Make sure you keep your knife close to the bones—do it slowly and watch what you're doing, so you don't remove anything destined to become bacon. Once you've separated the two, it's time to cook.

BACON

MAKES 5 POUNDS

2 cups coarse sea salt
1 cup whole black peppercorns, ground to a medium grind
1 (5-pound) skin-on pork belly
2 cups raw apple cider (preferably organic)

EQUIPMENT

7 cups hickory wood chips
Smoker box or heavy-duty aluminum foil

In a medium bowl, mix together the salt and pepper; rub the spices all over the pork belly. Put the pork belly in a shallow baking dish and drizzle with the apple cider. Cover and transfer to the refrigerator. Let chill for 24 to 36 hours.

Soak the wood chips in water for 1 hour before you plan to smoke your meat. Preheat the oven or grill to 210°F. Drain the wood chips and put them in a large metal container, or smoker box, set the container in the bottom of the oven or under the grate of your grill, and ignite the chips. If you are using aluminum foil, wrap chips loosely in foil, creating a packet, and punch a few large holes in the top. Place the packet in the oven or grill, and ignite chips. Be patient, especially if using an oven; the smoke may take a while to get going or be light.

Rinse the pork belly under cool, running water and pat dry with paper towels. If you're using an oven, fit a large roasting pan with a rack and set the pork belly on the rack. If you're using a grill, place the pork belly directly on the grill grates away from direct heat source. You want to smoke, not cook, the belly, and may have to work to keep the heat low and the chips smoking.

THE BEST WAY TO COOK BACON

How hard can it be to cook bacon? Too many breakfasts of burnt or soggy bacon have convinced us that not everyone has a deft touch when it comes to our favorite food. Bacon likes to be cooked over a medium flame, not incinerated on high. Cook it in a heavy pan—cast iron is a classic. Lay out your strips so that they touch the bottom of the pan fully but not each other. Bacon doesn't like to be crowded. Slowly heat the pan and flip the bacon occasionally to make sure it is gently crisping, not burning. Never drain the fat while cooking the bacon. When the fat starts to form tiny white bubbles around each strip, the bacon will be just right—not too crispy but not flaccid. Take it out of the pan and drain it. I like to do this on paper bags, but you can use paper towels as well. That's all that stands between you and a perfect BLT!

For a large crowd's worth of bacon, use the oven. Again, give the strips room on baking sheets (a Silpat liner is always nice but not necessary) and bake at 350°F for about 15 minutes. You can even go so far as to throw some brown sugar on top of the bacon before you put it in the oven—but that's gilding the lily.

One more thing: never, and I mean *never,* throw away your bacon grease. It is the essence of smoky, fatty goodness. You can use it in beans or corn bread, fry eggs in it, caramelize onions in it for a stew . . . the list goes on. Keep it in a glass jar near your stove or in the fridge—there's nothing that doesn't benefit from a little bacon grease.

When the wood chips are smoldering, put the roasting pan with the pork belly on the middle rack of the oven, or place the belly on the grill grates and cover the grill. Smoke the pork belly until an instant-read thermometer inserted in the thickest part of the meat registers 150°F, at least an hour per pound for lightly smoked bacon or longer for a smokier bacon. Remove the bacon from the oven or grill and let stand until an instant-read thermometer inserted in the thickest part of the meat registers 165°F.

Pull the skin off with your hands; it should peel right off in one big sheet. Slice and prepare the same as you would any store-bought bacon. Bacon can be stored wrapped in plastic wrap for up to 2 weeks in the refrigerator, or 6 months in the freezer.

FLEISHER'S SPARERIBS
SERVES 2

¼ cup coarse salt
3 tablespoons freshly ground black
    pepper
¼ cup packed dark brown sugar
¼ cup paprika
1 tablespoon garlic powder
1 tablespoon onion powder
1 teaspoon powdered mustard
1 teaspoon cayenne
½ teaspoon ground celery seeds

1 rack pork spareribs, poundage varies
    from pig to pig; ours tend to be
    around 3 pounds
Barbecue sauce, for serving (optional)

Make a spice rub by combining the salt, pepper, brown sugar, paprika, garlic powder, onion powder, powdered mustard, cayenne, and celery seeds in a small bowl. This makes about 1½ cups. Coat the ribs with the rub evenly and thickly. Don't be afraid of giving them a nice crust. Put the ribs in a container large enough to hold them, cover with foil or plastic wrap, transfer to the refrigerator, and let chill for 30 minutes to 12 hours.

We like to use an indirect method of cooking for the ribs, either slowly in the oven at 250°F for 3 hours—or until the meat pulls easily off the bone, whichever comes first—or at about the same temperature and timing on a gas or charcoal grill.

Cut the ribs apart and serve. We don't feel these ribs need anything more, but you can always serve them with barbecue sauce for dipping.

DRIVEWAY PIG ROAST

Come summer, it's pig-roasting time. We start getting the frantic calls for hogs around Memorial Day and they don't stop until almost Halloween. Here are a few things to remember when you want to roast a pig.

1. A pig roast is a true commitment.
In the early days of Fleisher's, a couple who became good customers and good friends asked us to do a pig roast for them. We said, "Sure, as long as you don't mind the fact that we are going to be in your yard at seven in the morning until seven at night drinking your beer, using your pool, and generally just scratching our butts. Oh, and by the way, we charge $100 an hour to do that sort of thing." They looked at each other and decided to grill some burgers and dogs instead. A pig roast is a long, slow process punctuated by waiting around, more waiting around, and an occasional flip or baste. If being "around" for at least 8 hours watching a pig sizzle is your kind of thing, there's nothing better. For a lot of people, the means don't justify the end.

2. Order early.
Most butchers don't have whole or half pigs lying around their shops. We order what we use weekly and don't usually have extras for chance walk-ins. Call ahead and we're happy to help. We sell fresh pigs; some butchers carry frozen ones. Make sure you ask and plan in advance how and where in your home you are going to defrost it (not at room temperature, please!) and give it enough time to defrost properly (it can take as long as three or four days).

3. Order a smaller pig than you think.
Only on one occasion has a pig ordered from us not been too big for the swarming, hungry masses. Usually people's leftovers overwhelm their fridge, their friends, and even their dogs. After drinking beer, snacking, and chilling for a full day, people are far less hungry than you might believe. We usually suggest a pound per person. So for 75 people a 75- to 80-pound pig is just fine.

4. Clear it with your wife.
I know I am being sexist here. I'm sure women roast pigs as well; I just have never had one ask me about it yet, maybe because women know it's going to be something of a hassle. I always counsel my customers to slow down, take a breath, and run the pig-roast plan by their wives before they confirm the order. Half of them never call me back. I'm never surprised.

5. Make sure you don't kill or maim anyone in the process.

Don't set your grass on fire, don't burn your roof, don't melt the asphalt on your driveway. You may think I'm joking, but we have heard tales of all of these (except the killing—I was just being dramatic).

6. Think about where you are going to store and carve the pig *before* you cook it.

This is a big piece of meat. It doesn't fit (easily) into a conventional fridge. We suggest brining a pig the day before a roast, but that means you must have a big enough space for the pig, the brine, and the ice. Most coolers won't cut it. We have heard of a kiddie pool filled with ice being used—we love creativity. Make sure whatever you use is clean and food safe. And make sure you have a whole table or counter dedicated to cutting up that pig once it is cooked. Don't forget tongs, a sharp knife, and plastic gloves so you can pull it apart the way nature intended.

Now, it's time to roast. Here are three methods we suggest.

❖ La Caja China or Chinese Roasting Box

This self-enclosed roaster/smoker can roast up to a 100-pound pig. Customers love that it's easy to use even in the rain. Check it out at lacajachina.com.

❖ Rotisserie, or Spit Roasting

Spit roasting seems to be the manliest way to roast a pig, which is already a pretty manly experience. You need the proper equipment, which can range from electric whole animal rotisseries (expensive!) to DIY bicycle rotisseries (nice!).

There are lots of websites devoted to building your own rotisserie, and you can rent one, but if you are going to buy new we like the ones at spitjack.com.

❖ The DIY Rebar/Concrete Block Method

This method is cheap, gives that true gritty driveway pig roast feel, and is damn efficient. It's also the one we are most familiar with. We can assure you it provides an excellent roasted pig every time. You literally build a pit out of concrete blocks, line it with aluminum foil, pile your coals on the foil, then throw rebar poles and two sheets of metal fencing on top of the poles. Your pig is trapped between the metal fencing, and you can flip it to your heart's content as long as you have a couple of buddies to help you. The Three Guys from Miami show you how to do it right at cuban-christmas.com.

Whatever method you go with, count on a long day. If you want to serve by 6:00 p.m. and you have a 150-pound pig, you need to start early in the morning. For a 40- to 70-pound pig, figure 4 to 5 hours, 70 to 80 pounds needs 5 to 6 hours, and 80 to 100 pounds takes 6 to 9 hours. This is a *very* inexact science. Don't forget to have enough charcoal on hand—at least 100 pounds for an 80-pound pig. Add more or less depending on the size of the pig. And remember, you don't have to do a whole pig to have a pig roast; you can buy sides or porchettas (fully deboned and weighing about 40 pounds that you can stuff or have your butcher do it). Or try spit roasting a bunch of shoulders.

Don't set your grass on fire, don't burn your roof, don't melt the asphalt on your driveway.

BEEF IS THE MOST POPULAR OF ALL OF OUR MEAT—and so iconically "American" that it might as well come in red, white, and blue. The meat cases are the first thing customers see when they enter a butcher shop, and laying them out is the most important thing a butcher does daily. The case is a canvas, a blank sheet. We nestle roasts next to steaks, wrap our skirts into rosettes, and scrape our rib chops so that the white of the bone provides a stark contrast to the raw, bloody beauty of the meat. And it's always the grind—rivers of it—that provides the focal point of our cases. When we paint our cases, it's just like a chef plating food at a restaurant—if it doesn't make your mouth water it's not doing its job.

ANGUS

A good case guides the customer, preempting questions. It should not intimidate or horrify (think pig head) or be conspicuously empty. An empty case forces customers to question freshness while a case that is poorly labeled does not elicit conversations. We know this from experience. When we first opened shop, we didn't label any cuts. We just filled our cases with whole primals, often thinly covered with plastic wrap. We quickly realized that expecting people to know what meat looked like and ask for what they wanted was a form of foodie arrogance. The plastic wrap was banished, the meat was displayed as if in a jeweler's case, and labels were printed. An abundant, well-lit, vibrant case is a butcher's asset.

The mountains of ground meat in the case are the most egalitarian. Everyone loves a burger, so that's what we have the most of. A wise butcher once told us you're only as good as your best ground meat customer. It's easy to sell steaks and roasts, but a steer is one-third trim—the odd but tasty bits of meat that we peel off bones and primals as we clean them, then use in our grind—so selling it ground is what keeps the meat moving and the butcher in business. The old lady who comes in once a week for ¼ pound of ground beef is our constant, the very heart of our community.

Grind is also the window into any good

DANGEROUS GRIND

Our loyal customers like to bring in newspaper articles dissecting recalls of E. coli–contaminated burger. Obviously we share their horror. It doesn't matter that there are USDA inspectors in every slaughterhouse. They're not catching the outbreaks and it's only getting worse. Contamination can come from anything—from feces on a hide to dirty hands to stomach bile that wasn't properly washed off a carcass. It takes time to slaughter and clean right. The giant operations rush to slaughter up to twenty-five thousand steers a day. When you see enormous numbers like 143 million pounds of beef recalled, it's because that's the "stop number": that's how much they grind before they clean or that's how many pounds ago they tested for pathogens.

butcher shop. If it doesn't taste phenomenal why is anyone going to spend $29.99 on porterhouse? Our grind is made with sirloin, round, chuck, and plate trim. It's the same muscle you might be eating for a steak or a roast, the same meat that fills the cases in different variations. It's ground daily and we mean it. Don't be fooled by meat labeled "freshly ground"

OUR DAILY GRIND

Ground beef, ground meat, hamburger, or as my grandmother used to call it, chop meat, is all one and the same. Grind, as we call it, is a standard 80/20 mix at the shop—that's an 80 percent meat to 20 percent fat ratio.

Most supermarket grind is far leaner than ours and often labeled with names rather than percentages: ground chuck, ground sirloin, and ground round. Although any cut of beef may be used for grind, the percentages are really what is being implied by these names: chuck is usually the standard 80/20 balance, while sirloin is a bit leaner, and round usually weighs in at 90 percent lean.

By law, the most fat that ground beef can contain if you buy it in a supermarket is 30 percent, but that doesn't mean you can't create some brisket-short-rib grind at home that might top the scale at 40 percent fat. Fat is flavor and truly decadent burgers are made with a fatty grind. We personally prefer a 70/30 grind. Remember, the fattier your hamburger is, the harder it is to prevent flare-ups on your grill.

THE PERFECT BURGER

If you like a flat top on your burger, use your thumb to make a divot in the middle of your patty. It will puff up as it cooks, giving you a nice surface on which to rest your (pastured) bacon, your heirloom tomato, and your local Cheddar. Pressing the burger flat while cooking makes the juices run out—don't do it. Kosher (or sea) salt liberally, then sear in a steel pan for 2 minutes per side, and transfer to a 325°F oven until it reaches your preferred doneness; check with a thermometer after 3 minutes in the oven. I like them bloody—I want it to look just spray-painted brown on the outside while still raw on the inside. The USDA suggests that you cook your burger until the internal temperature reads 160°F. That's because they want you to cook the shit out of it—literally! But remember, cooking does not destroy the prions that cause mad cow disease (nor does chemical disinfection or irradiation), and nothing can remove hormones and antibiotics.

at the supermarket. Usually that's a giant 20-pound chub (or tube) of coarse pre-ground beef they then *re*grind. That stuff is a gamble. There's no telling what's in it—bone chips and shit, at least. And it could also be made from a thousand different animals from ten different countries. Try tracing that.

Ground beef should taste like earth, sun, and grass and feel good on your tongue. We give some away to new customers who come through the door. I tell them, "If this doesn't taste like the best thing you have ever had, then don't come back." It's a risk, but it always works.

Our grind plus tongue, tail, and everything in between all come from pastured, hormone- and antibiotic-free steers on five or six farms near us. Our guys do their own on-farm breeding or buy from local cow/calf breeding operations. They don't buy random auction animals and then raise them as their own. This traceability is crucial to us, especially when it comes to mad cow disease. Our animals' all-vegetable diets also decrease the likelihood of mad cow. The trouble begins when you turn ruminants into carnivores and give them feed containing diseased animals.

One of our slaughterhouse guys is also a farmer who raises about two hundred cattle a year—mostly for Fleisher's—and he helps us procure the rest. He only kills ten to fifteen a week (remember, a conventional slaughterhouse does up to twenty-five thousand a day). We do five a week in the winter and about seven a week in the summer, including restaurant sales. This currently adds up to a little over three hundred head a year. So we need multiple farms to make sure we have enough to sell. Over the years we have figured out that we do best with farms with at least sixty steers. That couple selling beef at your local farmers' market may do only five a year. We love small farmers, but to fill our cases weekly with their meat, we would have to deal with a hundred of them. A quality pastured product is a slow one. Our steers take their sweet time getting to slaughtering weight—anywhere between twenty and thirty months. Like humans they all grow at their own pace to different sizes. Five on the ground doesn't mean five ready to slaughter. Inevitably we would fall short—and wipe out their whole herd. Working with that many small farmers would also create insurmountable consistency issues.

Ground beef should taste like earth, sun, and grass and feel good on your tongue.

OF GRASS AND GRAINS

Our pastured animals never eat any meat or meat by-products, but most do eat some local grain along with grass, plus hay, balage, and silage. The grain (usually ground local corn) gives the meat good flavor and helps the animals maintain their weight during the winter when there's no grass on the ground. Since we opened shop, we have also occasionally offered 100 percent grass-fed meat in season, which, unlike our standard, comes from steers who never ate any grain. This distinction sometimes confuses people. Both animals are pastured, but one eats some grain, and one eats only grass. If we lived elsewhere, we might be able to offer both year-round. But in New York's Hudson Valley, 100 percent grass-fed beef is (mainly) only available fresh from August through December; frozen, obviously, is available year-round. During the winter, and even in fall and spring when the grass isn't growing, all pastured animals eat hay, balage, and silage. The ones fed 100 percent grass that get no additional grain maintain but don't gain weight. They're slaughtered either before winter or once they're back on grass and gaining again. Fresh, 100 percent grass-fed beef in the winter is a rare bird. That said, some producers do slaughter in the winter, especially in the South or on the West Coast; they have shorter winters.

If you've never considered how much grass or grain your steak contains, you may be wondering what the big fuss is about 100 percent grass-fed animals. They've been getting a lot of attention in sustainable food circles these days. The current thought is that it's best for the animal, especially ruminants, to eat their natural diet exclusively. When they do, their meat is said to have more nutrients than when they're eating grain, including omega-3 fatty acids and CLA (conjugated linoleic acid—a "good" fat that has exhibited cancer-fighting properties in some studies). But our business is meat, not vitamins. We're happy to stock 100 percent grass-fed beef when we have access to it, but in our experience it isn't for everyone. It's truly lean, with a deep, earthy flavor that can be a bit much for some people. Old agriculture journals show that livestock has been given corn for well over 150 years; Americans have been raised on grass- and grain-fed meat and it's what their taste buds are used to. It's a fattier product, with a milder flavor than 100 percent grass-fed. Our sales indicate that most customers prefer a little grain.

GRASS

HAY is grass that has been mowed and then dried. Because it is of limited nutritional value, farmers also feed their animals silage and balage.

SILAGE AND BALAGE are grasses or plant materials and their stalks that are cut fresh, partially dried, then baled or placed in a silo and allowed to naturally ferment. They are used for feed usually when grass is not growing during the winter, spring, and fall seasons. The lactic acid that is produced during this fermentation process helps to preserve the silage, aids in digestion, and adds nutritional value.

BY ANY OTHER NAME

The word *cow* gets thrown around for anything that moos. But technically, cows aren't what produce meat; they're the milk makers. Sometimes you might eat an old dairy cow ground into burger or sausage, but mainly steer is what's for dinner. If you want more general terms to toss around, you can say "cattle" or "beef cattle." Here are the specifics.

BULL A male with all of his parts, a breeder

CALF A male or female less than a year old

COW A female that has had a calf or calves

HEIFER A young female, not yet a mother

STEER A castrated male

BREEDS

Animals are bred and crossbred for growth, climate, yield, fat content, food conversion (how much feed they need to grow), and susceptibility to disease. Our beef comes from Black or Red Angus, a very popular American breed, or Angus crosses. They're hardy and do extremely well in harsh Northeastern winters. Angus are bred for meat—they look like a block of steak held up by four tiny toothpicks. They have solid genetics, a high carcass yield (that's the ratio of meat to fat to bone), and good fat in the muscle (marbling) as well as on the exterior (the fat cap).

PASTURED VS. ORGANIC VS. CONVENTIONAL

There is a monumental number of beef cattle here in America. As detailed in "The Backstory" (see page 31), not all are raised equally. Far from it. Avoiding conventional beef is crucial, but guess what: not all small-farm pastured beef is raised equally, either. Generally speaking, these animals are outside their whole lives on rotating pastures. Sometimes those pastures are sprayed to keep weeds down, sometimes not. Some small farmers may administer growth-promoting hormones to their animals or antibiotics, though usually only if they're sick (see page 227).

MAKING THE GRADE
When consumers buy steak, they think and ask about grades—mainly prime and choice. Remember that pastured steers aren't graded or categorized for their intramuscular fat content (see page 55).

BEYOND OUR BREEDS

Throughout the years farmers have offered us everything from Texas Longhorns (our slaughterhouse couldn't even fit the horns through the door) to Chianinas, an Italian steer that does double duty as a draft or work animal, whose meat is about as tender as you would imagine it to be. We are breed-centric and we prefer to stick with what we know, but here's a short list of other breeds you may come across when shopping for pastured meat.

BELTED GALLOWAY We call these Oreo Cookie Cows; they are black with a white band running around their middle. Sweet and docile, they seem to be a favorite among gentleman farmers (farmers who are not dependent on their farm for their livelihood)—after all, who wouldn't want a hillside dotted with these cuties.

DEVON (RED OR BLACK) Known to gain well on 100 percent grass, this steer is very popular among pasture-based farmers. They were probably the first purebred cattle to come to North America.

HEREFORDS This is one of the most popular breeds because they fatten up quickly and have a good meat-to-fat ratio. You'll recognize the iconic red steer with a white head and chest that, along with Longhorns, shows up in paintings of the Old West. Most of the time these fellows also have horns, but there is a polled (hornless) variety as well.

HIGHLAND This adorably shaggy Scottish steer does very well—for obvious reasons—in extremely cold weather and on a 100 percent grass diet. This is the Royal Family's beef animal of choice, and they keep a large herd of them at Balmoral Castle.

SIMMENTAL These big boys are often crossed with smaller breeds for their positive characteristics like docile personalities and a high carcass yield.

Others don't. Some small farmers may "finish" their cattle—fatten them up before slaughter—in small feedlots. Others won't. Some animals are fed supplementary feed that may or may not contain genetically modified grain. The only way to know how your pastured animal is living, what it is eating, if it has been given drugs, and how it has been finished is to ask questions when you are shopping. We suggest great things to ask about in Sourcing (see page 218). You also need to educate yourself enough to understand the answers. Buying certified organic, for example, will mean that the animal was never administered drugs or given feed containing animal by-products or waste, pesticides, or anything genetically modified, but it doesn't guarantee much beyond that. There are certainly large factory organic farms that grain-finish in feedlots, and they might not be anywhere near where you live. We always prefer well-raised local pastured meat to organic, but obviously organic is vastly preferable to conventional.

AFTER SLAUGHTER

Steers are massive, up to 1,500 pounds; our average carcass weighs 850 pounds. They hang at our slaughterhouse for 7 days, then get cut into four primal pieces per side (eight total per animal) before we bring them into the shop—arm chucks (shoulders/arms), ribs (uh, ribs), loins (midsection beside the ribs), and leg. These parts can weigh between 70 and 210 pounds per piece. They're skinless but very hard and dry on the outside, with a nice fat cover that dries out as you age it. This becomes that delicious, crispy-creamy band of fat on your steak. The slaughterhouse sells hides and offal to buyers. We do get heart, liver, tail, tongue, and sometimes "oysters" (like "fries," a euphemism for testicles, but most of our animals are castrated steers, not bulls). In our business, time and weight are money. We start losing cash at the moment of slaughter. Our animals are sold at hot hanging weight and it's all downhill from there. When a steer is killed, the carcass—minus head, hide, and internal organs—is immediately thrown into a blast chiller. This lowers the body temperature and keeps bacteria from thriving while the carcass is being cut. Even before we pick up animals from the slaughterhouse we lose up to 4 percent of the meat as the carcass goes from hot to cold. At five a week and current prices that's $22,000 lost in the chill over one year—just for steers.

DRY AGING AND WET AGING

After that initial week hanging at the slaughterhouse, we continue to dry-age loins and ribs up to twenty-eight days and legs for a week. Arm chucks are broken down immediately. Dry aging is one of those buzzwords that makes everyone excited. In laymen's terms it's "controlled rot." Sounds disgusting, but what it does to the muscle—softening it and concentrating the flavor—is truly a beautiful thing. Jessica likes to say that all the foods she loves the best are fermented in some form or another—wine, cheese, pickles, and beef. Obviously she is not alone. Only around 25 percent of an animal is dry-aged for a full month. These high-end primals line our coolers in various states of decomposition, each covered in a fine, downy blanket of mold. This bacteria—similar to that which makes cheese so delicious or penicillin so powerful—is trimmed off before the steak is sold, leaving only its telltale musky, earthy taste. But with trim comes more loss—up to 25 percent of each of these primals ends up in the trash. That's money out of the butcher's pocket. Dry aging *is* expensive, which is why large packinghouses don't do it and why it costs more for the consumer. When you dry-age you need to do it correctly; this is not a process you can stop and then restart. Constant temperatures and circulating air are necessary to dry the meat correctly and form a tough outer shell with no real decay.

Conventional beef, on the other hand,

NOTE TO MEAT COWBOYS

Dry aging is not the type of thing you can do at home, and if you are, please don't tell us; it gives us heart palpitations. Every time you open your fridge for a beer (and someone who is trying to dry-age his or her own porterhouse is just the type to be reaching for one frequently), you are raising the temperature of your cooler. You need a cold, dark place that is visited infrequently and huge cuts of beef to make this work well, otherwise you are going to be left with a tacky, moldy, stinking, and dangerous mess. If you feel like you *must* dry-age at home we suggest buying a chest freezer, hanging your loin from a bar suspended in the cooler, and turning the temperature to somewhere between 35°F and 38°F. The humidity needs to be at 50 to 60 percent. Invest in a good thermometer and a gauge to read humidity. You can also buy dry-aging coolers. And do the research before you get started. Either do it like a professional or leave it to the professionals.

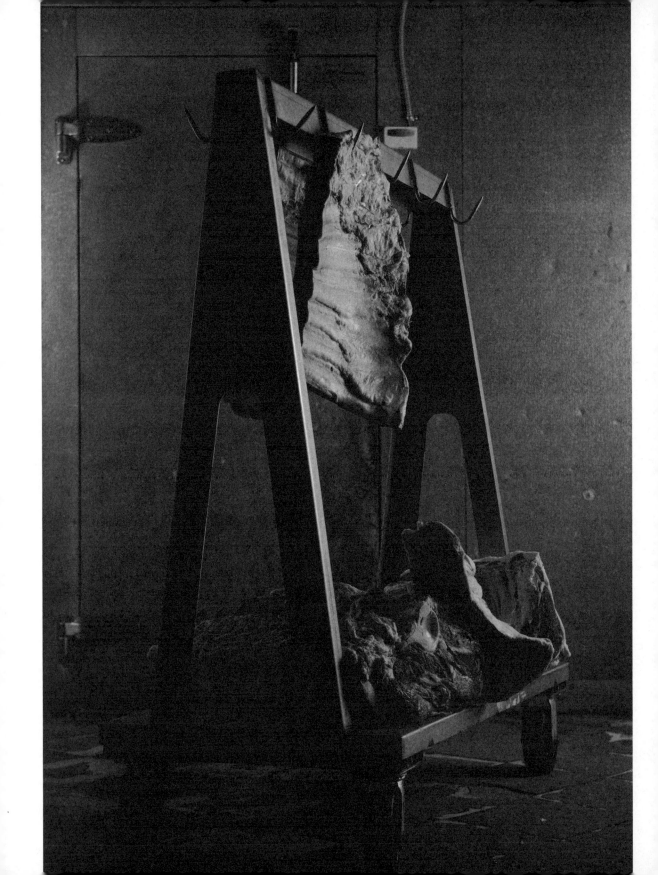

is "wet-aged" in vacuum-sealed plastic bags. As the meat begins to bleed out, or "purge," it sits in pools of its own blood liquid and becomes wet-aged. Meat can sit in those bags for weeks or even months without spoiling. This method does cause muscle to break down and become softer, but it does so without that umami flavor that dry aging imparts. Though we don't have much experience with conventional meat, we do taste tests as part of our apprentice program. It's amazing what you can learn about your own meat by looking at and tasting someone else's. Conventional product feels and tastes different from pastured beef for many reasons. Our apprentices always notice that conventional steaks fail to crisp the way ours do, that the muscle is mushy and flaccid, lighter in color, and less flavorful.

Dry aging reduces the moisture content of the muscle. This makes it tender and juicy when cooked, and the surface forms a delicious crust—one of the hallmarks of a perfect steak in our book. Pastured steaks literally have muscle. Poking one is like poking a ripped guy in the chest: your finger bounces back instead of sinking into a doughy mass. This has to do with how the steer was raised. The more it strolled around the farm, the tighter its muscles will be. The best steaks are deep red. Lighter-colored flesh indicates the age of the animal—ours are usually between twenty and thirty months old, while conventional animals are alive for only a short year. The different flavor is a factor of the breed, the way the animal was raised, what it ate, how old it was when it was slaughtered, how that meat was aged, and how it was cut.

PRIMAL PRIMER

As we've been explaining, steers are really large animals, usually between 1,000 and 1,500 pounds live weight. A 1,500-pound animal will produce a carcass of about 850 pounds, of which 85 percent is usable meat, bone, and fat. Seasons, feed, and genetics all influence a steer's yield. A carcass is categorized into two sides, and each side yields two quarters: the front half, called the forequarter, and the rear, known as the hindquarter.

At Fleisher's, we have the slaughterhouse cut the carcass in half, then divide it into four basic primals per side. From the forequarter come the arm chuck and the rib. From the hindquarter come the loin and the leg (conventionally this is called the round).

The *arm chuck* weighs from 100 to 200 pounds and comprises the entire shoulder section, including the first through fifth ribs. This is a heavily worked muscle grouping, and it contains more connective tissue than other regions, so most of the cuts coming from this area require a low, slow method of cooking like braising. This is also the area that provides the most amount of ground meat per animal.

The *rib* is one of the two most highly prized sections of the steer. It weighs 65 to 110 pounds and reaches from the sixth rib, adjoining the arm chuck, to the twelfth rib, nestled next to the loin. (There are thirteen ribs in each side of a steer's body, twenty-six in all, and the thirteenth rib stays in the loin.) The rib runs along the animal's back and includes higher-priced cuts that are generally grilled, seared, or roasted.

The *loin* weighs in at 55 to 100 pounds and runs from the end of the ribs to the steer's tush (round). It's filled with highly flavorful, very popular cuts. This is where the money meat comes from, so this primal is the most expensive.

The *leg* (aka round) is 65 to 90 pounds and comprises the entire upper rear leg and includes the shank (on a human this would be the shin), making it a giant drumstick. This primal contains the femur and aitchbone (hip socket) and provides the best marrow bones. The leg is made up mostly of "rounds," which are tasty but lean and tough—ideal for roasting and braising.

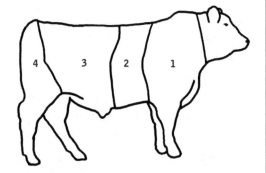

BEEF PRIMALS
1. CHUCK
2. RIB
3. DROP LOIN
4. LEG

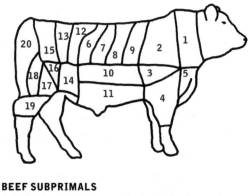

BEEF SUBPRIMALS
1. NECK
2. CHUCK EYE
3. SHOULDER CLOD (TOP BLADE, TERES MAJOR, FLATIRON)
4. SHANK
5. BRISKET
6, 12, 13. NEW YORK STRIP
7. DELMONICO (FIRST CUT RIB EYE)
8. RIB EYE
9. RIB ROAST/PRIME RIB
10. SHORT RIBS
11. FLANK
12. T-BONE
13. PORTERHOUSE
14. SIRLOIN FLAP (FAUX HANGER)
15. SIRLOIN TOP
6, 12, 13, 15. TENDERLOIN
16. TRI-TIP
17. SIRLOIN TIP
18. EYE ROUND
19. SHANK
20. TOP ROUND

Cook This Way

CHUCK This section is known for inexpensive cuts.

> **Brisket**—braise or smoke or corned for pastrami
>
> **Chuck eye roast**—roast
>
> **Chuck steak**—stovetop to oven (see page 90) or braise
>
> **Ground meat**—any cooking method or raw
>
> **Knuckle bones**—stock or dog bones
>
> **Marrow bones**—roast or stock or dog bones
>
> **Neck meat**—braise
>
> **Shank**—braise
>
> **Short ribs**—braise or grill
>
> **Shoulder clod/flat iron**—stovetop to oven or grill
>
> **Stew meat (fatty)**—braise
>
> **Teres major (we call it faux filet)**—stovetop to oven or grill
>
> **Top blade or chicken steak**—sear

RIB These tasty inexpensive cuts and delicious high-end steaks are the best of both worlds.

> **Boneless rib roast or prime rib**—roast
>
> **Ground meat**—any cooking method or raw
>
> **Hanger**—stovetop to oven or grill
>
> **Inside skirt steak**—stovetop to oven or grill
>
> **Outside skirt steak**—stir-fry
>
> **Rib eye steak (aka Delmonico, cowboy steak)**—stovetop to oven or grill

> **Rib roast**—roast
>
> **Stew meat**—braise

DROP LOIN The most popular cuts reside here.

> **Flank**—stovetop to oven or grill
>
> **Ground meat**—any cooking method or raw
>
> **New York strip (aka shell steak)**—stovetop to oven or grill
>
> **Porterhouse**—stovetop to oven or grill
>
> **Sirloin flap/fajita steak**—sear or grill
>
> **Tenderloin (aka filet mignon, filet, Chateaubriand)**—roast or stovetop to oven or sear
>
> **Top sirloin toast**—roast
>
> **Top sirloin steak**—stovetop to oven or grill
>
> **Tri-tip**—stovetop to oven or grill or roast

LEG A great source for large dinner-party-type roasts and lean stew beef.

> **Bottom round roast**—roast or braise
>
> **Eye round roast**—roast or dry-cure (see page 180)
>
> **Eye round steak**—sear
>
> **Ground meat**—any cooking method or raw
>
> **Knuckle bones**—stock or dog bones
>
> **London broil/top round steak**—stovetop to oven or grill
>
> **Marrow bones**—roast or stock or dog bones

Shank—braise

Sirloin tip roast—roast

Sirloin tip steak—stovetop to oven or grill

Steamship round (whole leg including shank)—roast

Stew meat—braise

Swiss steak/bottom round steak—pan-sear

Top round roast—roast

It takes a while to work through a steer. It's the most intensive and detailed work a butcher does. Half a steer should be carved up in about forty-five minutes. (Half a pig, on the other hand, I can do in forty-four seconds.) You don't want to plow through it; you want to be careful, to focus. My arms ache after a while; it's tough on your body. Muscles are actually finely seamed together, layered one on top of another, and can be pulled apart easily with just a little pressure and a sharp knife. You don't need to be a big burly man to butcher. Size can help when you're ripping an animal apart with your bare hands, but we've taught tiny women who can barely reach around a leg of beef to butcher. Women are often better than men at finessing rather than muscling their way through sides. Jessica likes to compare butchering to rock climbing.

PLATING
At home we never serve a steak without slicing it first. We do this for a number of reasons: When we have guests it gives them a chance to get a piece of their choice—some like it rare, some medium. It also stretches the steak: when sliced portions rather than one large hunk of meat are offered, people (us included) take less and eat less. Smaller pieces are easier to eat; you never have to deal with bone or gristle. We just pile the bones (if there are any) on the side and let the true carnivores chew on them for dessert.

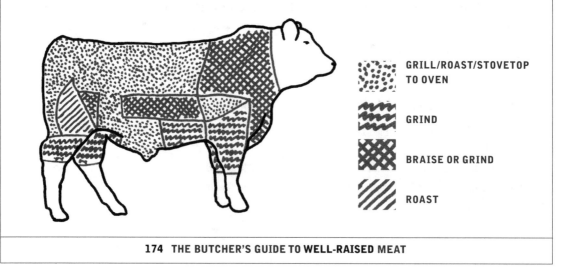

GRILL/ROAST/STOVETOP TO OVEN

GRIND

BRAISE OR GRIND

ROAST

COOKING THE PERFECT STEAK

Unless you pay close attention, grilling is perhaps the quickest way to ruin pastured beef. It is always leaner than its conventional cousins, requiring a delicate balance of heat and timing, and a lot less latitude as far as cooking times go. You can't throw it on the grill and walk away. Grilling may be sexy, but we beg, we plead, we cajole customers to follow our instructions: pan-sear and finish it in the oven. Our favorite steak is dry-aged top sirloin at least 1½ inches thick. With a thinner steak, don't transfer to the oven.

❖ Preheat the oven to 300°F.

❖ Bring to room temperature, then salt each side of the steak and let it sit for 5 to 10 minutes before cooking.

❖ Heat an ovenproof pan (French steel or cast iron is preferred) over high heat until it starts to smoke (oil is not necessary, but add a tablespoon of organic canola oil if you like).

❖ Sear the steak in the hot pan for 2 minutes per side. (Never use a fork to turn the steak; use your fingers or tongs.)

❖ Put a splash of olive oil, a pat of butter, a dollop of bone marrow, or a mixture on top of the steak.

❖ Transfer the pan to the oven.

❖ Cook for 4 to 8 minutes to desired doneness (it depends on the steak, so go by internal temperature, not time—we recommend 120°F for a perfect medium-rare).

❖ Take the pan out of the oven, place the steak on a cutting board, and let it rest for 5 minutes.

❖ Slice and serve.

YOU CAN'T ALWAYS GET WHAT YOU WANT

We are a sustainable butcher shop. That means we use every part of the animal. The term *nose to tail* gets used a lot and mostly we are able to do that, though it's easier with a pig and harder with a steer. Pigs lend themselves to that process because they come in a much smaller package. Beef is trickier, even though it's our most popular meat, just because there's so damn much of it. The top-end cuts—your rib eyes, strips, sirloins, and tenderloins—sell themselves. Briskets, short ribs, and the rest of the lovely braising meats sell well in the winter or to intrepid summer smokers. The midrange meats like top round, which we make into London broils, plus hangers, flank, and skirt are a constant—everyone wants them. The subprimals like bottom round sometimes have fewer takers, but we can always make them into roast beef (see page 183). Since we must sell every last bit of beef, we have had to come up with ways to move *everything*. Our frozen patties, meatballs, hot dogs, and beef sausages help us deal with the surplus.

The most difficult thing about being a sustainable butcher is not having every cut available all of the time. Take the hanger steak. In recent years, the hanger—aka the butcher's tenderloin—has become prized by people who like a tender, moderately priced, and deeply flavorful steak. Unfortunately there is only one per animal. If we have five steers in a week to work with, we sell five hangers—that's all, folks, until next week. We spend a lot of time explaining this to new customers. Eventually they get it. You *should* want us to sell out. It proves that we're doing what we say we are. If you go to a restaurant and see hanger steak on the menu, it's not a sustainable restaurant, no matter what

THE BUTCHER SUGGESTS: BEEF SHANKS

Veal shanks are prized as osso buco and lamb shanks as, well, lamb shanks, but what about the lowly beef shank, aka shin meat? It's inexpensive, flavorful, and incredibly tender when cooked properly. One of our favorite cuts, it's a great base for a meaty soup like Vietnamese pho or for Texas-Style Beef and Chile Stew (see page 186). Get your butcher to cut the shanks osso buco style for maximum marrow removal.

THE PERFECT STEAK
(page 175)

BRESAOLA
(page 180)

ROAST BEEF

(page 183)

BITE-YOUR-TONGUE TACOS
(page 185)

FLANKEN (OR SHORT RIBS),
FLEISHER'S STYLE
(page 188)

HEART
(page 63)

FLEISHER'S "SECRET" CHICKEN RUB
(page 216)

JAPANESE FRIED CHICKEN
(KARAAGE)
(page 212)

BRICK CHICKEN
(page 211)

they claim. They aren't buying whole animals and using everything. Those hangers come in a box. We would be the first in line to buy a steer made up of hangers, tenderloins, and strips, but that just isn't how they're configured, and we work with what nature created. Thankfully beef can be cut in lots of different ways. As we've said, the Germans cut differently from the French who cut differently from the Americans. There are also regional and even shop-specific cuts. To help ease the hanger situation, we went searching for a cut that chewed like a hanger but was more readily available. The "faux" hanger was born: it's the flap from below the sirloin. There are two per animal. At other shops, flap meat is used as stir-fry meat or turned into grind. At Fleisher's, it's one of the most popular cuts. We sell it right alongside our skirts, flanks, and regular hangers. Sometimes you *can* get exactly what you want—if you are a little flexible.

THE NAME GAME

If you find yourself standing in front of a case confused by names, you're not alone. There are an infinite number of steaks in a steer, and what they are called, once cut, is largely regional. So it's important to know that what you're actually asking for is a sirloin or a rib eye, even if it has different names. Speak up and ask questions so you can make sure you get what you want no matter what part of the country you're in.

Here's what we call some common steaks, along with what they might be called elsewhere:

FLANK STEAK Also called bavette, arrachera, "stir-fry" beef

NEW YORK STRIP, BONE-IN Also called bone-in top loin steak, sirloin strip steak, strip steak, club steak

NEW YORK STRIP STEAK Also called boneless top loin steak, strip steak, boneless club steak, Kansas City steak, Ambassador steak, shell steak

RIB EYE STEAK Also called Delmonico steak, market steak, cowboy steak, rib steak

TENDERLOIN Also called filet mignon, filet de Boeuf, filet, Chateaubriand

Confused? Allow us to confound you further. There's the additional issue of terms like *London broil,* which refer to the thickness of the cut or a type of cut, not specific parts. We take London broil from the top round, so we should advertise them as top round London broils. But we don't always. Another butcher might use a chuck eye for London broil. The same goes for pot roast, which is a cooking method, not a steak or a cut. We like a nice chuck eye for this, but any braising cut can be used.

THE REAL VEAL

Veal is so controversial. Due to a brilliant campaign on the part of animal rights activists, it has been off the plates of most people who care about how their dinner was treated for quite some time now. The biggest problem with veal is obviously the way in which the calf is raised, most often in a plastic "hut" and chained to a stake. This should preclude anyone from supporting the commercial veal industry. But for most dairy farmers in this country, veal is part of the way they can turn a profit. What else are dairies going to do with surplus male calves? Only a few are needed for breeding. Most dairy breeds—Holstein, Guernsey, Jersey—aren't generally raised for beef, which makes them less valuable in the industry and certainly not profitable to feed. For most dairy farmers, killing male calves young is the best solution for utilization.

But we know those huge, limpid, chocolate eyes are the real reason that people have trouble eating veal. "I don't eat babies," our customers cry as they turn away from the case, shuddering. Guess what? When you are eating our pork, lamb, or chickens, you *are* eating youngsters as well; they are just not as cute. Lambs are slaughtered at ten to fourteen months, pigs at nine months to a year, and chickens squeak by with a mere three months. Veal is usually four to six months for milk/formula-fed, and six to twelve months for rose veal—more of an adolescent steer than a baby. Conventionally raised animals have an even shorter life span. Animals that we eat, in general, are not long for this world.

We carry veal only infrequently, most often from farmers who have let the calves nurse and roam free. They have not yet eaten a blade of grass, which is what is meant by the term "milk-fed" veal. In the past we have also carried rose veal. Either way, it's veal. Keep in mind that every time you have a chai latte, eat a piece of milk chocolate, or even wear lipstick (which often contains tallow), you are supporting the dairy industry, which in turn contributes to and supports the veal industry. It's a system. We aren't telling anyone to give up the cream in their coffee. We're just eager for people to see the symbiotic relationships all foods have with one another.

Home Fabrication

Home chefs eager to stick their knives into a steer in their kitchens are largely out of luck. It's not like you can just take a 200-pound arm chuck home from the farmers' market and put it in your fridge until you're ready to deal with it. But there are plenty of fun things to do with more manageable pieces of beef at home.

EYE ROUND TWO WAYS: DIY BRESAOLA AND ROAST BEEF

Both of these recipes use the same exact cut, one 3- to 5-pound eye round, cleaned of silver skin, fat, and sinew. The eye round, or eye of round, is from the steer's hindquarter (in the middle, near the aitchbone), which means it is extremely flavorful but too tough to make a good steak. That also means it's inexpensive. In most butcher shops, it is a neglected cut of beef that often ends up in lean ground meat or as stew meat. Not in ours. Here's what we do with it.

BRESAOLA

Bresaola is one of the few cured beef products that we make in the shop. If you're not familiar with it, it's an Italian air-dried, cured (and by that we mean salted) beef stick. We cold-smoke our bresaola briefly for just a hint of flavor. Cold smoking is a process that smokes meat without exposing it to heat, usually at temperatures between 85°F and 110°F to bring out complex flavor. Cold smoking, like larding (covering a curing meat with lard), or peppering, is an ancient technique.

Unlike hot smoking, which is how we cure our bacons, hams, hocks, and chops, cold smoking can take days or weeks to complete, and it tends to yield drier, saltier foods.

Since cold smoking does not technically cook or extensively cure the meat, cold-smoked meats are usually brined or salted before smoking. Salting the meat ensures that bacteria will not develop during smoking and storing. That said, cold smoking provides the perfect conditions for bacterial growth, which is why some people add nitrites (see page 142).

In his book Charcuterie, *Michael Ruhlman suggests 1 ounce per 25 pounds of meat; you do the math based on the size of your eye round. Ideally cold smoking should be done in the fall and winter. We are extremely careful to take every safety precaution when we cold-smoke, and you should, too.*

After we smoke our bresaola, we hang it in our coolers for 4 to 5 weeks. As it ages it turns dark, almost inky in color, and develops a deep red center. We slice it paper-thin and suggest our customers serve it like carpaccio (another favorite): give it a splash of olive oil, a hit of pepper, and a squirt of lemon. Slicing meat paper-thin at home can be a real bitch if you don't have a deli slicer (we realize not everyone keeps one in the basement). Use those extraordinary knife skills you have been honing to shave whisper-thin slices with a long, thin prosciutto knife.

❖ **MAKES ABOUT 2 POUNDS**

1 (3- to 5-pound) eye round, cleaned of
    silver skin, fat, and sinew
10 pounds coarse sea salt (you need
    enough to cover the eye round)
InstaCure #2 (optional; see opposite and
    pages 142–143)
¼ cup finely ground black pepper

EQUIPMENT
Butcher's twine
2 cups aromatic wood chips, such as
    hickory or cherry
1 cup beer, water, or cider, for soaking
    the wood chips
Smoker box or heavy-duty aluminum foil
Small refrigerator, such as a dorm or
    beer fridge
Medium-size nonreactive container

Before you begin, find a nonreactive
container large enough to hold the eye
round and small enough to fit in the
refrigerator.

Salt the eye round by rolling it in salt
until it is entirely covered. Then bury it
completely in salt in the container.
Refrigerate it at 38°F for 4 days.

Take the eye round out and wash it
under cool, running water to remove all
the salt. Pat dry with paper towels. Roll
the eye round in the pepper until it is
completely covered. Tie it like a roast
with butcher's twine (see page 94) and
make a loop on one end to use for
hanging the meat.

Soak the wood chips in the liquid of
your choice for 1 hour. Drain the wood

chips and put them in a smoker box or loosely wrap them in heavy-duty aluminum foil and punch out a few large holes. Place the box/foil packet in the bottom of your oven or under the grate of your grill and ignite the chips. Do not turn on the oven or grill. Cold smoking imparts flavor, not heat, so actually "cooking" the bresaola is not the goal here. The smoldering smoke from the damp chips gives flavor. (Some grills come with special fancy-schmancy smoking drawers with burners—if you have one of those, follow the manufacturer's instructions.) Place the eye round on the grate of the grill or on the bottom rack of the oven and cold-smoke for 2 hours.

Remove the eye round from your grill or oven. Let it come to room temperature, then hang it from its twine loop in a refrigerator that is set at about 40°F. This should *not* be done in the fridge you use daily, as the opening and shutting of the door will throw off the

temperature, which must remain constant.

When the strings surrounding the round become loose and the meat becomes dry and slightly leathery looking, after about 30 days it's ready. Slice and serve.

MOLD VS. MOLDY

Many cured meats develop mold as they age. White mold is fine; it's a naturally occurring tasteless spore that actually shows that the curing conditions (temperature, air circulation, and salinity) are spot-on. If your meat is covered in green or black mold, throw it away. Do not under any circumstances try to "salvage" it by washing it or scraping it down. It is not worth it. This type of mold is reflective of the fact that the cure was not strong enough or that it was stored in a cooler that was too warm or too moist or both.

ROAST BEEF

A perfect roast beef is a thing of beauty. It is simple, economical, and delicious. Roast beef is great for sandwiches, or throw together some sort of mustardy-horseradishy concoction and serve it to your friends instead of prime rib. One eye round is great for a family of four for one meal plus a couple of days of leftovers for sandwiches. Roast beef should last for about five days in the refrigerator—the meat will still be delicious and safe to eat, though it won't look as perfect as it did on day one. We don't recommend freezing roast beef as it will dry out considerably and look unappetizing.

❖ **SERVES 4 WITH LEFTOVERS**

1 (3- to 5-pound) eye round, cleaned of
    silver skin, fat, and sinew

3 teaspoons kosher salt

1½ teaspoons freshly ground black
    pepper

3 tablespoons vegetable oil

1 medium onion, sliced into ½-inch-thick
    rounds

4 garlic cloves, lightly crushed

6 (2-inch) marrow bones

3 tablespoons unsalted butter, sliced into
    thin pats

½ cup beef or chicken stock (preferably
    homemade) or white wine

A crusty baguette

Preheat the oven to 350°F.

Tie the eye round with butcher's twine (see page 94). Season generously with salt and pepper.

In a large roasting pan set over high heat, heat the oil until it's almost smoking. Sear the roast on all sides until it has a good brown crust, 4 to 5 minutes per side. Transfer the roast to a plate and set aside. Add the onion and garlic to the pan and cook, stirring, until browned, about 5 minutes. Settle the bones among the onion and garlic, arranging them into a rack. Put the roast on top of the bones and onion, then scatter the butter pats over the top of the meat. Add stock or wine to the bottom of the pan, making sure that the liquid does not cover the bones. Transfer the roasting pan to the oven and cook for 35 minutes, basting every 15 minutes or so with the pan juices and the stock.

The roast is done when an instant-read thermometer inserted in the thickest part of the meat registers 120°F for medium-rare. Remove the pan from the oven and let it rest for 5 to 10 minutes before slicing. The roast can be served hot or at room temperature. Spread the marrow from the bones on bread to accompany the meal.

RACK ATTACK
Oh no! You don't have a roasting rack but you do have a roast (or a chicken) that is just begging to be cooked. Try our method: build one out of food. Our favorite is marrow or knuckle bones, but we're the only ones we can think of who have *those* lying around the house. The marrow adds flavor to roasts and then you can use it as an accompaniment or make marrow "butter." I push the marrow out of the bones with my fingers, coarsely chop it, melt it in a little butter, and drizzle it on my steak before I put it in the oven. But I'm just bad that way. Most folks have carrots, celery, or onions on hand, so create a tower with them to keep the meat out of the grease and juices.

CHINE ON
When you order a bone-in roast (whether beef, lamb, pork, or veal) from your butcher, make sure you get the chine bone—which is butcher talk for spine—removed with a band saw. This will allow you to cut the roast into individual chops or steaks. If you are feeding a crowd you might want to think about having your roast hinged. This is a simple process (so simple you can do it at home) in which the butcher cuts the full roast off the bones and ties it back on. If you want to do this before dinner, simply take your 5-inch knife and run it down and along the ribs (not between), neatly severing the connection between meat and bone. Keep the meat nestled securely against the ribs and tie a piece of twine around it. Then tie string between each rib to fully secure the roast to the rack. In this way, the meat benefits from being roasted "bone-in" but you have a roast that you can cut cleanly and easily into different-sized portions. It goes without saying that you should remove the twine before you serve it; slice the roast at the table for an extra flourish and to receive those accolades.

Our favorite is marrow or knuckle bones, but we're the only ones we can think of who have those lying around the house.

BITE-YOUR-TONGUE TACOS

Shred tongue and serve on warm tortillas with a dash of salsa verde and some fresh cilantro leaves and thinly sliced radishes. ❖ **SERVES 4 TO 6**

1 tongue (about 2½ pounds)
1 tablespoon salt

Rinse the tongue under cold water and make sure it is clean. Put the tongue in a large stockpot with enough room so that it doesn't touch the sides. Cover with water. Bring to a boil over medium-high heat, then cover the pot and lower the heat to low to keep a good, solid simmer. Let simmer for 3 hours; the tongue is done when a sharp knife pierces it easily and the membrane looks ready to slide off.

Remove the tongue from the pot and let cool on a plate for about 15 minutes. It should be cool enough to touch but not so cold that the membrane sticks. Peel off the membrane and clean the underside of the tongue of any tough bits. You may need a sharp knife.

Put the tongue back in the stockpot, add the salt to the water, and bring to a boil over medium-high heat. Cover and lower the heat to low to keep at a simmer. Simmer about 1 hour, until the meat is tender and can be pulled apart easily.

SALSA VERDE

This is our favorite sauce, given to us by Juan Pablo Lopez, our sausage maven, who has been with us from the beginning.
❖ **MAKES 3 CUPS**

1 pound fresh tomatillos (11 or 12), husked
2 to 3 jalapeño peppers, to taste
1 garlic clove, chopped
¾ teaspoon salt
1 ripe avocado, diced
½ cup finely chopped white onion
¼ cup chopped fresh cilantro

Put the tomatillos, jalapeños, and garlic in a medium saucepan and add ½ cup water. Set the pan over medium heat. Bring the mixture to a boil, reduce the heat to low, and simmer, uncovered, for about 15 minutes, until the tomatillos are soft and have lost their vibrant green color. Drain, reserving the liquid, and let the vegetables cool.

Transfer the cooled vegetables and liquid to a blender. Add the salt and puree on high speed until smooth. Pour the mixture into a bowl and stir in the avocado, onion, and cilantro. Cover and refrigerate for 1 hour, then adjust the seasoning if needed.

TEXAS-STYLE BEEF AND CHILE STEW

This is a riff on a delicious lamb stew recipe that our friend/bouchère/writer Julie Powell made for us one very memorable Christmas Eve. The evening was unforgettable for many reasons, but the stew figures most prominently in all the stories that surround that night. (Adapted from the El Paso Chile Company's Texas Border Cookbook.*)* ❖ **SERVES 6**

8 mild green chiles (preferably a combination of New Mexican and poblano; adjust the amount of peppers depending on the type of pepper and the intensity of their heat)

5 to 6 tablespoons olive oil

4 pounds bone-in beef shanks, cut into ½-inch-thick pieces and well trimmed

2 cups chopped onions

3 jalapeño peppers, stemmed, seeded and minced, to taste

4 garlic cloves, minced

2 teaspoons dried oregano, crumbled

4 cups beef stock (preferably homemade)

1 (35-ounce) can organic crushed plum tomatoes, drained

1½ teaspoons salt

2 pounds boiling potatoes (we like Carolas), peeled and cut into 1-inch chunks

12 corn tortillas, warmed, for serving

Position a rack in the lower third of the oven and preheat the oven to 350°F.

Using the flame of a gas burner or a broiler, roast the chiles, turning them so that they are lightly but evenly charred. Place them in a paper bag, close the bag tightly, and steam the peppers until they are cool enough to handle. Rub away the charred skin. Stem and seed the chiles, then cut them into ¼-inch-wide strips. Set aside.

Meanwhile, heat 2 tablespoons of the oil in a 5-quart nonreactive Dutch oven or stovetop-to-oven casserole set over medium-high heat. Working in batches, add the shanks to the oil and sear them, turning occasionally until well browned, about 4 minutes per side. Add an additional tablespoon of oil to the pan if it gets dry. Transfer the browned shanks to a bowl.

Reduce the heat to low, add the remaining 3 tablespoons of oil to the pan, and stir in the onions, jalapeños, garlic, and oregano. Cover the pot and cook, stirring occasionally and scraping the browned bits from the bottom of the pan, until the onions are soft and golden, about 5 minutes. Stir in the stock and tomatoes. Return the beef shanks to the pot and season with salt. Bring the stew to a boil, then cover the pan and place it in the oven. Bake for 45 minutes, stirring once or twice. Stir in the potatoes and roasted green chiles, and bake, covered, for another 45 minutes, stirring occasionally, until the beef is falling off the bone and is extremely tender. The stew should have thickened slightly. Adjust the seasoning and remove any remaining gristle from the bones. Cut up any large chunks of meat before serving. Serve with warmed tortillas.

FLANKEN, FLEISHER'S STYLE

We marinate very few things at the shop; we don't want to overmarinate and lose the true flavor of the meat. We prefer that our customers do it themselves. Flanken (or short ribs cut Korean barbecue style) is one of the few exceptions. It takes well to marinating, so you can leave the ribs in the marinade for up to 12 hours without losing that big, beefy taste.

Flanken has a funny place in our hearts. It appeals to both our Jewish sides and our foodie natures. Most older balabustas, *or Jewish housewives, know flanken (a Yiddish term for flank, or side) as a flavorful, inexpensive cut to be braised. A good Jewish cook didn't dare serve borscht without a good chunk of flanken in it to add that earthy, rich feel. For years we were traumatized by this cut; older Jewish women would walk into our store and order flanken. We would say, "Short ribs, right?" and get berated. Sometimes we would be able to convince them that we were talking about the same thing. It's the same bones, but a different cut—flanken is cut horizontally across the rib plate so that you get long, thin pieces of meat studded with many ribs. More recently foodies have been ordering this cut and grilling it Korean style. They call it* kalbi. *Given the choice between borscht (which, according to my grandmother's recipe, is meat cooked until it is tasteless accompanied by mushy beets) and* kalbi, *I go Korean every time.* ❖ **SERVES 4**

---

4 to 6 garlic cloves, minced

1 (1-inch-long) piece fresh ginger, peeled and grated

½ cup soy sauce

½ cup mirin

¼ cup rice vinegar

¼ cup canola oil

2 tablespoons pure maple syrup

2 tablespoons toasted Asian sesame oil

1 tablespoon Asian chili sauce, such as Thai Sriracha or Korean gochujang

3 pounds flanken, cut 1 inch thick, 2 to 3 ribs across

¼ cup chopped fresh cilantro

2 tablespoons toasted sesame seeds

1 teaspoon kosher salt

1 head butter lettuce (optional)

¼ cup coarsely chopped scallions (white and green parts)

Put the garlic to taste, ginger, soy sauce, mirin, vinegar, canola oil, maple syrup, sesame oil, and chili sauce in a bowl and mix well. Pour the marinade into a thick, sealable bag, place the flanken in the bag, and marinate for 30 minutes at room temperature, or up to 12 hours in the refrigerator.

Heat a grill to high. Oil the grill grates. Remove the meat from the marinade and put it on the grill; reserve the marinade. Grill the meat until done, about 3 minutes on each side. Be careful not to burn the ribs; the high sugar content of the marinade makes them char easily. Transfer the ribs to a platter and set aside.

Pour the reserved marinade into a saucepan set over high heat. Bring it to a boil and cook until it becomes thick and syrupy.

To serve, drizzle the flanken with the reduced marinade and sprinkle with the cilantro, sesame seeds, and salt. To eat, pull the meat off the bones, wrap it in lettuce leaves if using, and sprinkle with scallions.

POULTRY

N ONE OF THE FIRST FEW DAYS WE WERE OPEN, a guy burst through the door and stomped over to the counter. After considering the cases for a moment, he looked up and said, "What's wrong with your chicken, man? It's not yellow!" He looked down again and then stalked out. Yellow? we thought to ourselves. Yellow chicken? Slowly it dawned on us that conventionally raised chicken is often yellow from the dyes added to poultry feed. Raw poultry *should* range from bluish white to pink to pale yellow. But in this guy's mind a good fresh chicken was a bright yellow bird and not the pale, glistening specimens in our cases. Though that scene was never repeated, it made us realize that we Americans believe our chicken should be as yellow as Tweety Bird just as we believe that every table should be graced with a 25-pound turkey on Thanksgiving. These iconic images have somehow worked their way into our mass subconscious. And though beef might be the most American of all our foods, chicken is the most homey. Imagine Sunday dinners without the ubiquitous roast chicken, picnics without fried drumsticks, or the flu without soup. When you picture a steak you think of a cowboy, but when you picture chicken you think of mom. Chicken is a comfort food for everybody, probably even those cowboys.

This is why we put our rotisserie right in the window of the store, so the first thing that hits you as you walk through our door is the smell and sight of roast chicken. It was my idea to put it there. Jessica thought it was déclassé, but then she saw how much customers love it. People hover in front of the store to watch the birds spin. It's like chicken TV. They're our most powerful sales tool—covered in an organic spice rub Jess created, snapping and crackling as they go round and round on their absurd Ferris wheel. Everyone comments on them, everyone buys them—that's the idea. We sell out *every day*. People even put in standing orders with us. See page 216 for our (no longer) secret rub recipe.

Beef may be the centerpiece of any shop, but the butcher knows that chicken runs the show. It's the common denominator. All customers—even people who come in for offal—buy chicken: breasts, legs, thighs, whole birds, and more breasts. Luckily, even before we opened our doors, we recognized America's love affair with the bird and sought out a large, organic chicken producer so that we could keep up with demand.

WANT LOCAL PASTURED BIRDS?

What's fresh in our cases all comes from the same organic producer, but we often have whole local pastured chickens in our freezer at the shop, and are happy to tell interested customers about regional farms that do sell consistently tasty, fresh pastured chickens. During summer months, when the Kingston Farmers' Market lines Wall Street in front of our door, Jessica sometimes wanders out and gets a pastured chicken from a farmer we know. Our customers think it's funny. She likes the flavor and doesn't mind the chew. She brines them, soaks them in buttermilk, and fries the hell out of them. Who wouldn't love that?

PASTURED VS. ORGANIC VS. CONVENTIONAL

Yes, you read that right: chicken is the only certified organic animal we carry—whole birds and parts. We know this may come as a surprise since we've been saying for pages now that while organic meat is a vastly superior, highly preferable choice over conventional supermarket fare, we prefer—and exclusively stock—local pastured lamb, pork, and beef. But chicken is a different, well, bird. We're running a business. When it comes to giving customers the chicken they want—consistently flavorful, not too gamy, and in parts—at an economical price, USDA organic was the best choice for us. How we arrived at the chicken we currently sell is a tale of painstaking sourcing.

In 2004 we started out thinking we would sell only local pastured birds. We did the legwork. We went to the farms. At one well-regarded, highly recommended farm that was selling at many, many New York farmers' markets, we found no birds—no animals at all. It was quiet and not for any of the right reasons. We were particularly interested in this farmer because he had a state-inspected slaughterhouse facility on his property, meaning he could sell to us. (Due to USDA Agricultural Marketing Service rules too complicated and dull to describe here, most small farmers can slaughter their birds on their farms and sell them in farmers' mar-

kets, but not to butcher shops.) But this guy clearly wasn't even producing enough chickens for the amount he was selling at farmers' markets, let alone if he was going to start wholesaling to us. He was obviously getting his birds elsewhere—a traceability no-no. Years later we found out that he was kicked out of the very same farmers' markets for what amounted to fraud.

This experience reinforced our commitment to always visit farms, even ones recommended by people we trust. But it was also the writing on the wall. We realized that no one local farm, no matter how perfect it might appear, would ever have enough chickens to sell to us. Our weekly orders were—and are—too high. In order to sell pastured poultry, we would have to rely on several different farms with big enough flocks to make our numbers and have them slaughtered at a federal facility, which would be logistically and financially impossible. Whole birds, we could swing. But Americans don't want to buy only whole birds; they have a never-ending, undying, and bizarre obsession with boneless skinless chicken breasts. In France, maybe, but not in Kingston. Our customers want parts, but local pastured birds come whole, and they're very rarely processed into parts at the slaughterhouse. The numbers work for us to do the cutting for a 1,000-pound steer, but it's too expensive for us to buy whole birds, then spend the time and manpower to cut them up and still sell them at a reasonable price. People consider chicken to be an inexpensive protein and balk at paying higher prices than they're used to.

Besides price, pastured birds present a consistency issue. American palates are used to the taste of confinement birds, not the texture or flavor of their pastured brethren, which must be cooked carefully or they go chewy. One overly rubbery bite and we easily lose customers. So we went in search of a certified organic producer capable of meeting our weekly demand for whole birds (mainly for the rotisserie) as well as boxed parts. Beyond organic, our requirements were that the birds be raised as close to the shop as possible, that they be free-range (this requires less space than for a hulking steer), and that they consistently taste delicious. We lucked out. Our free-range certified organic birds come from North Carolina; they eat certified organic corn and soybeans, as per USDA regulations; they are never given growth hormones, antibiotics, or animal by-products; and they're damn tasty.

We realize there's a whole other realm of so-called natural free-range chickens on the market, many of them the secondary lines of some of the country's largest conventional chicken producers. These birds are stocked by many stores that sell "sustainable" food. The standards for them aren't strong enough for us. Even though they may not be given antibiotics (and never hormones, because the government bans hormone use in all poultry), "natural" ain't the same as organic. Even natural free-range chickens can be fed the most disgusting slop you have ever imagined, nothing you would choose to put in your mouth: postslaughter animal waste from factory-farm beef, lamb, and pigs, plus feathers and manure as well as arsenic (yeah—the same thing that poisons humans promotes growth and inhibits illness in birds). So why the hell would you want to eat something that was raised on it?

Conventionally raised factory-farm chickens, besides being fed the garbage described above, are beyond bleak, and buying them should never be an option.

Americans don't want to buy only whole birds; they have a never-ending, undying, and bizarre obsession with boneless skinless chicken breasts.

Genetically engineered for meat to the point where their breasts are so big they can't even walk, stacked in cages thousands upon thousands together, beaks sheared off so they can't peck each other, living in their own excrement (and receiving manure burns all the while) and sickened by its chemical fumes—it's worse than you could ever imagine for them, the workers, and the environment. And for us, if we eat them.

AFTER SLAUGHTER

Our birds—whole and parts—are freshly killed, usually within two to three days of when they arrive. They're never prefrozen. We can tell by looking at the bones: if they have been frozen, you'll see red spots. Vessels in the marrow burst if you freeze them; ice crystals are sharp. We also get fat (for sausage) and bones (for stock). Occasionally we run into supply problems and we can't always get what we need—but that's okay. As we've said, unlimited supply in this industry is a dead giveaway that someone is full of it. We're constantly trying to get our customers to understand that when we're out of something it means we're doing what we say we're doing—it's a sustainability barometer.

We eye, feel, and smell every delivery. Chicken should be firm—you should be able to push into the muscle and have it bounce back. Fresh skin is slippery smooth, never sticky or tacky, and it should adhere to the muscles. Some parts might be detached slightly, but you shouldn't be able to take your fingers and go underneath the skin. There's a coating of fat there and we look for it to be pretty thick. You can always tell how much fat a bird will have by squeezing the pope's nose—the bottom of the back where the tail is. The fatter the ass, the juicier the bird. (We'd like to use this space to own up to and apologize for the fact that for the first three years of Fleisher's, there was not one rotisserie chicken that went out our doors with its butt. Jessica, a die-hard pope's nose fan, ate them all. Guilt stopped her eventually.)

While chicken is the most pedestrian of meats, it seems to bring up the most issues. We have plenty of customers who buy chicken because they don't think of it as meat. You might have run into these so-called vegetarians at a dinner party—they tell you all about why they don't eat meat as they reach across your plate to snag a wing. When did chicken become a vege-table? And there are others who consider chicken to be diet food. We're happy to cater to anyone, but unless you're eating a boneless skinless chicken breast cooked in little to no fat (yawn), you're better off with a grass-fed London broil. That said, there's nothing quite like a skin-on roasted chicken leg. Live a little.

SIZE MATTERS

Oddly American consumers buy only certain sizes of chickens. No one asks for a 7-pounder or a 2-pounder. Why the hell not? For the life of us we cannot fig-ure it out. There's nothing *wrong* with a broiler that weighs something other than 3 to 5 pounds. But demand influ-ences supply. For us it's bizarre, but for the contract growers—farmers hired by packinghouses or producers on a con-tract basis to grow their birds on their feed to a specified weight in a certain pe-riod of time—it can be devastating. The growers—conventional *and* organic—can really get screwed by our size-ist system. Say they grow the birds to the right specs, then arrive at the processing plant only to discover that they're not buying that week because wholesale orders are down. If this happens, a farmer has only two options:

1. Use gas/time/energy to haul the birds back to the farm and feed them more, losing money on an extra week of feed (chickens are notorious pigs). It's proba-bly no picnic for the birds to make the trip, either. Then lose more gas/time/energy transporting those same birds back to the plant the following week only to be paid less per pound for them. Ironically bigger birds cost less per pound—they are worth less because consumers don't want them.

2. Kill the birds and bury them. It's cheaper. More farmers do this than you'd like to believe.

So, the next time you're buying a whole chicken, try being a little more flexible and not so uptight or wedded to a recipe that calls for a specific weight. Tweak the recipe. Eat less. Or make more and have leftovers.

BY ANY OTHER NAME

If, standing before a meat counter, you see names like *poussin* or *stewing foul,* you might think these are different birds. They're not. These are classifications. Here's what they mean. Thanks to our mentor, the butcher and Culinary Institute of America professor Thomas Schneller, for letting us lift this from his textbook *The Kitchen Pro Series: Guide to Poultry Identification, Fabrication, and Utilization.*

POUSSIN Small, sold whole; 1 to 1.5 pounds; three to four weeks old

CORNISH GAME HEN Small, sold whole; 1 to 2 pounds; four to five weeks old

BROILER/FRYER Midsize, sold whole or in parts; 2.5 to 4.5 pounds; six to ten weeks old

ROASTER Large, sold whole or in parts; 5 to 9 pounds; nine to twelve weeks old

CAPON Large, castrated male, sold whole; 5 to 9 pounds; nine to twelve weeks old

HEN/STEWING FOWL Large, female egg layer past her prime, sold whole; 4.5 to 7 pounds; more than ten months old

ROOSTER Large, male, sold whole, a rare find; 4 to 8 pounds; more than ten months old

KEEPING IT CLEAN AT HOME

All this talk about disinfecting should make you think about how you're doing it at home. Chicken needs to be washed before you cook it, even if it's organic. Organic has nothing to do with cleanliness. Here's how to do it:

❖ Place a colander in the center of the sink, and put the chicken in the colander. Rinse with cold water (heat makes bacteria reproduce, so cold is your friend) to remove any nasty stuff.

❖ Move the chicken to where you'll prep it. Sterilize the colander and the sink. At the butcher shop, the health department requires us to use a bleach solution. This is a very small amount of bleach diluted in water—half a cap per gallon of water that we then test with pH strips to check the levels. People use far too much bleach. Read the bottle instructions and *dilute* with cold water, as bleach dissipates in hot water. At home, we use bleach, too, but vinegar or a hydrogen peroxide-based "green" cleaner works just as well.

❖ Clean all surfaces or utensils that have had contact with the poultry post-prep.

HANDLE WITH CARE

We take serious precautions to avoid cross-contamination between different kinds of meat. Home cooks should be doing this, too. Beef, pork, and lamb are cut on the same table here at the shop, but chicken is relegated to totally separate cutting boards in a separate area. In the walk-ins, chicken is never open to the air the way other meats are. Chicken parts are washed daily. In our cases, it's the only meat covered in plastic. People think we do this to avoid contamination, but we actually do it because poultry dries out fast and then looks unappetizing. We keep chicken only for a week and beyond that it is used for dog food. Whatever surface poultry touches is sterilized.

Chicken is cleaned before it even makes its way to the shop. The U.S. government requires poultry to be sanitized prior to selling to rid it of things you would rather not serve for dinner, like salmonella, E. coli, and campylobacter. Poultry is chilled after it has been de-feathered and eviscerated to reduce the likelihood of those very things reproducing and to preserve freshness. This tends to be done by sticking untold numbers of carcasses at once into giant vats of constantly refreshed freezing water, where they commingle and swap bodily fluids. To minimize cross-contamination, some places add disinfectants to the water.

Depending on where you live, some antimicrobials aren't looked on too kindly. The European Union has long banned the use of chlorine baths to sanitize food. And back in 2007, when the Brits were discussing lifting a ban on importing U.S. chicken, citizens called for chlorine-bathed birds to be labeled "Treated with Antimicrobial Substances" or "Decontaminated by Chemicals." Pretty funny. Can you imagine that flying here? USDA organic standards don't permit chlorine in amounts above what's already in all of our drinking water. Birds can also be air-chilled, or hung separately out of water so they don't cross-contaminate, eliminating the need for a disinfectant.

PRIMAL PRIMER

Despite the fact that we buy and sell chicken parts, customers of course ask us to cut up whole chickens. We oblige, but cutting up a chicken is the sort of thing anyone can—and should—do at home. All you need is a 5-inch knife and maybe some poultry shears to crack the chest bone. There's really no need for a primal primer for poultry; it's well known that birds break down into quarters (two leg/thigh combos and two breast/wing combos) or eighths if you are going wild (two legs, two thighs, two breasts, two wings). There are endless possibilities of what you can do with your broken-down chicken—or even a whole one. We consider it the pasta of the meat world—a vehicle for sauce, it can take on any flavor. This is both the reason we love chicken and its greatest crime. In meat and foodie

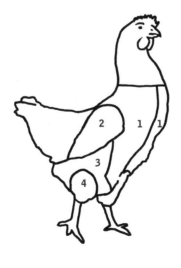

CHICKEN PRIMALS
1. BREAST
2. WING
3. THIGH
4. LEG

circles, chicken is much maligned as dull. When I asked my staff, who are not great chicken lovers, what it is that they *do* love about the bird, this is what they said: "the bones and the skin"; "the crunch and the fat"; "the fact that I can cook it over a can of beer"; "slow-braising it in honey, wine, and prunes" (sweet mother of God!); "confiting it in lard." (And you thought I was decadent.) They may claim not to always love it, but they sure as hell know what to do with it.

In meat and foodie circles, chicken is much maligned as dull.

TURKEY

Perhaps no other animal at the shop elicits more tales of woe than the turkey. No matter that we only sell the bird during the holidays; holidays make everyone—customers and butchers alike—lose their minds. Think of how stressful it is to gather all you need for your family's Thanksgiving dinner. Now multiply that by getting those birds together for hundreds of Thanksgiving dinners. Here's the thing: we sell only pastured fresh turkeys. This complicates the nightmare. You cannot tell by looking at a young bird how big it will be, and you cannot stop it from growing until you slaughter it. Most people purchase a frozen bird that happens to have been killed at their desired weight. But to sell fresh birds means slaughtering mere days before Thanksgiving—five at most, between a traditional Saturday slaughter and a Wednesday pickup. In other words: we have a horrible time matching customers with the size bird they desire. Sure, you can find "fresh" birds of all different sizes at a supermarket, but there's no way of knowing if these are truly fresh. Nor are they raised on a small local farm; only factory-farm birds can be produced in such massive quantities that you can get an exact size. Your "fresh" turkey could be three weeks dead—bleached and vacuum-sealed to make it appear fresh—and you would be none the wiser. Yet another reason to have a butcher you trust.

Admittedly we've gotten better at this turkey *mishegas* over the years—we had to, after our first year, when we commissioned a pair of novice gentleman farmers to grow four different kinds of heritage turkeys. The idea was that each kind would grow to a different size, so we'd be able to get everyone their preferred poundage. Big. Mistake. We wound up giving a 28-pounder to a woman who had ordered a 12-pounder. Incredibly, she didn't freak out, which is why she's a friend (and loyal customer) to this day. Other people didn't react as well. We have seen women sobbing over something 2 pounds too small. Now we put a disclaimer on our turkey order forms. It states that there is a four-pound margin of error on either

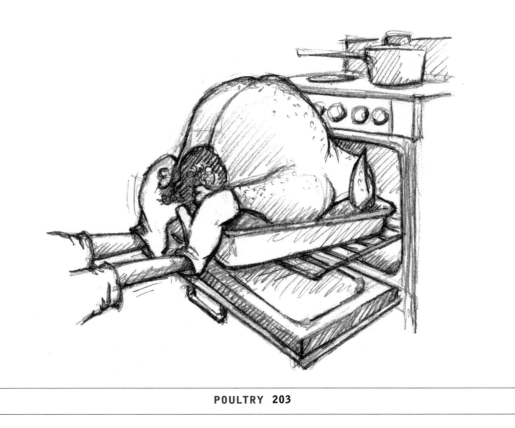

DUCK, DUCK, GOOSE

We usually don't sell geese or squab or pheasant. We can't compromise what we do so we just don't do it. We reserve the right to change our minds if and when the right suppliers come along. One of our pig farmers recently offered to grow game fowl for us, so we'll see. We have duck on and off when we can get it, usually frozen (unusual for us) Pekins from Long Island. (*Pekin,* by the way, is a type of duck, like mallard, Muscovy, or Duclair. *Peking* duck is a dish.) Our customers ask for duck often, so we like to carry it. There's less of it out there than chicken; they're farmed differently. Ducks need free-ranging access to pasture and water. They do well on bugs, not just grain. They're older when slaughtered. When contemplating duck, choose a recipe that calls for the whole bird: using only a bunch of legs isn't very sustainable. Don't forget to prick the skin well so the fat drains off, and make sure your oven is clean—unless you want the fire department to come for a surprise visit.

side. Sometimes it's even more variable. If you can't handle the stress of not knowing exactly what your turkey is going to weigh, do *not* order a pastured bird. That said, we encourage you to take the risk. There is a reason we sell out every year: they taste phenomenal.

If it's not the customers making us crazy, it's the predators. In 2009 thirty of our birds were eaten by a raccoon family before we could have them slaughtered. We had to cobble together replacements but only had six left to sell for Christmas, the only time we do sell frozen birds. Jessica begged to spend the following

holiday in Canada, where they don't celebrate Thanksgiving in November.

For all of these reasons and more, turkey is a seasonal product for us. We'd actually like to sell it out of season, but no local farmers are raising turkeys except to sell for the holidays. Pastured, heritage birds take longer to grow than chickens—five or six months—so farmers have to start planning months in advance. We start getting calls in April and May to inquire about how many we might want for Thanksgiving. Growing turkeys year-round is just something our farmers don't want to contend with.

Pastured, heritage birds take longer to grow than chickens—five or six months—so farmers have to start planning months in advance.

THE (UN)COOPERATIVE SYSTEM

The majority of egg and poultry producers in this country work within a cooperative system. Though the term *co-op* brings to mind hippies and good-for-you grains, the reality is anything but. The way that these co-ops work is that a poultry or an egg producer moves into a rural area and sets up a processing facility. What could be wrong with that? Farmers get to do what they have been already doing and now they can sell their product to a company that has set up a local processing facility. Well, here's the rub: When the producer moves in, they contract with, let's say, ten farmers (contract growers) to raise chickens or produce eggs for them. The producer gives these farmers both the genetics—which are proprietary—and the feed. They can never buy their own chickens and are locked into buying feed at the price that the producer decides to charge them. Each contract grower is expected to come up with a certain amount of product per week and bring the product to the processing facility. Part of the deal is that they're only allowed to sell chicken or eggs to the producer (too bad if they aren't buying that week) and at a price the producer sets (can you say serfdom?). The worst part for the consumer is that all of these chickens or eggs are sharing the same genetics and feed, and if there is anything wrong with either—like disease or pathogens in the chicken feed—the problem is ultimately being shared among thousands and thousands of birds. Hence, the massive recalls that we as consumers experience.

EGGS

We have been carrying eggs from local pastured hens since opening shop. They don't have to be certified organic, but they do have to be pastured (i.e., no fencing and they can go wherever they want to go) or at least be extremely free-range and given certified organic feed. Seventy-five percent of chickens in America are kept in cages. The farms we buy from come and go because chickens sometimes stop laying. One guy, whose chickens were traumatized by weasels, played classical music to soothe them, but they still wouldn't lay. Sometimes we barter with producers—their eggs for our meat. We look for yolks that are bright orangey yellow; this means they're eating exactly what they should be eating. Some "farmers" who keep their chickens in cages dye the yolks via the feed so they appear pastured. We have the real deal. Most conventional eggs you buy at the store will have pale yellow yolks and thin shells.

We run out of eggs just like we run out of hanger steaks. Sorry. But it shouldn't come as a surprise. This is what happens. It's part of the sustainable/local/seasonal game. Chickens lay more eggs in the summer than they do in the winter. Supply ebbs and flows naturally. Around the holidays, when people are baking up a storm and chickens are producing less, you might find yourself in front of the cooler where we keep the eggs, out of luck. These things happen. Be flexible.

We charge somewhere around $6 for a carton of eggs. People used to buying a dozen for a couple of bucks might find this outrageous. Stop for a minute and consider the difference between the life pastured chickens live—scratching and pecking around between dirt baths and laying at will—and that of their conventional counterparts—cramped by the thousands in cages, stinking beyond your wildest imagination, eating God knows what, and efficiently dropping eggs like machines. And think of the workers. Then six bucks actually seems like a bargain. What else can you eat for breakfast that's a buck? A bagel? A dollar meal at McDonald's?

Home Fabrication

Unlike lamb, pork, or beef, cutting a whole chicken yourself is a manageable endeavor. Cooking at home is a lot easier if you know how to break one into eight pieces. Plenty of home chefs are already comfortable doing this. But learning how to debone a skin-on breast or remove a spine can be a snap. It might even get your poultry repertoire out of a rut.

CUTTING UP A CHICKEN

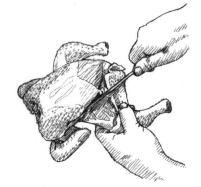

This is not rocket science. Follow the bird's natural seams. They will be your guide. There are several ways to do it, none are wrong. Here's one.

❖ Place the chicken, breast side down, on a cutting board. Grab the leg and pull it away from the body. Slice through the skin between the breast and the leg/thigh.

❖ Keep pulling the leg until it pops out of the socket and is exposed. Cut next to the ball severing the leg/thigh from the body. Repeat on the other side.

❖ Lay the bird on its side and pull the wing. Slice through the joint between the wing and the breast to remove it. Repeat on the other side.

❖ To separate the breast from the back, slice between the rib cage and the shoulder joints and remove. You now have the whole breast.

❖ Turn the breast over so the skin side faces down. Break the backbone by hand, then cut through using a knife or poultry shears. If you want to cut the breast in half, this is the time to do so.

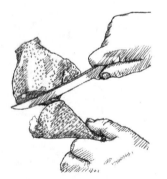

❖ To separate the leg from the thigh, pick it up and break the joint with your hands. You will hear the pop. Then slice cleanly through.

❖ The finished product.

BUTTERFLYING A CHICKEN

Butterflying (or spatchcocking, as the Brits say, don'tcha just love that word?) a chicken is a lot easier than it sounds. You're just removing the backbone and splaying it open like a book.

Remove the spine with a pair of poultry shears (Jessica's method) or a sharp knife (mine). After you remove the spine, flip the chicken over and with the heel of your hand press down on the breastbone hard enough to break and flatten it. Throw the spine in the freezer for stock. And you're ready to cook. We suggest brick chicken.

Marinate the chicken or not. Brush it with oil and sprinkle with salt. Sear the now spread-eagle chicken in a smoking-hot pan skin side down, and cover with a brick or two wrapped in aluminum foil to weight it down. If you don't have a brick (apartment dwellers, you know who you are), use a heavy skillet. Flip the chicken after 10 minutes, and cook the second side for another 10 minutes. Next, transfer the chicken and the bricks to a 350°F oven for 30 minutes.

Remove the chicken from the oven and place it on a cutting board; put the pan on the stovetop. Deglaze the pan with a little butter, stock, and white wine. (Okay, I go a little crazy here and use bacon grease and pork stock but that is not for the faint of heart.) Cut up your chicken, drizzle with pan gravy, and serve to an appreciative audience. Next time, try it on the grill.

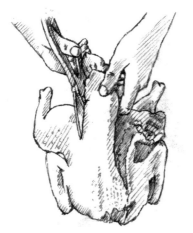

JAPANESE FRIED CHICKEN (KARAAGE)

Jessica loves fried chicken. If she were on death row and requested her last meal, it would defi-nitely be fried chicken and biscuits. She's not even southern. This is her version of the perfect food with an Asian twist. I love this recipe because it uses boneless skinless chicken thighs, which are so flavorful, and because these nuggets are cooked in lard—always a good thing. Lard gives the chicken a crispy, crunchy crust without burning. ❖ **SERVES 4**

¼ cup soy sauce

¼ cup mirin

2 teaspoons peeled minced fresh ginger

2 garlic cloves, minced

1½ pounds boneless skinless chicken
   thighs, cut into bite-size pieces

⅓ cup all-purpose flour

⅓ cup cornstarch

½ teaspoon kosher salt, plus more for
   sprinkling

¼ teaspoon freshly ground black pepper

¼ teaspoon ground sansho pepper
   (optional)

½ pound block lard, for deep-frying

⅛ teaspoon shichimi togarashi (optional)

Lemon wedges

In a small bowl, combine the soy sauce, mirin, ginger, and garlic. Add the chicken thighs, toss well, and marinate for at least 20 minutes and up to 30 min-utes at room temperature or up to 4 hours in the refrigerator.

In a medium bowl, combine the flour, cornstarch, salt, and black and sansho peppers if using. Working with one piece of chicken at a time, remove the chicken from the marinade and drop it into the seasoned flour mixture. Shake off any excess flour and place the chicken on a plate. Repeat with the remaining chicken thighs. Let the chicken sit until the coating is absorbed and the color changes from white to light brown, about 5 minutes.

In a deep skillet or wok, heat enough lard so that the chicken pieces will be completely submerged to 330°F. Test the temperature of the lard by dropping a pinch of dredging mixture into the oil. If it sizzles immediately on the surface without burning, it's ready. Fry 5 or 6 pieces at a time, cooking until the crust is lightly colored, about 1 minute. Transfer the chicken to paper towels or a metal rack and let drain.

Lower the temperature of the cooking oil to 310°F; it's ready when a pinch of dredging mixture sinks slightly when dropped in the oil before sizzling. Fry the chicken a second time in batches for 3 to 4 minutes, until golden brown. Do not let it get too dark. Transfer the chicken to paper towels or a metal rack and let drain. Sprinkle the pieces with salt and shichimi togarashi, and squeeze some lemon juice over the top. Serve immediately or at room temperature.

CHICKEN LIVER PÂTÉ

The recipe for this easy chicken liver spread, or pâté, comes to us from our good friend Matt, who was one of our first customers. We call it Maté, in his honor. In the early days of the shop he offered to make it for us and our customers. He found the recipe in a book given to his wife, Stephanie, by the owner of a bookstore in Florence while they were on their honeymoon. At first the owner didn't believe that Matt was the cook of the family, accepting it finally in only a bemused sort of way. Matt, who is also the creator of Mattwurst, a garlicky French-style sausage we sell, is a gifted cook. ❖ **SERVES 8**

---

3 tablespoons extra-virgin olive oil, plus more for drizzling

2 carrots, finely chopped

2 medium onions, thinly sliced

2 celery stalks, finely chopped

1 pound chicken livers

¼ cup dry red wine

¼ cup chicken stock (preferably homemade)

8 anchovy fillets (if salt-packed, rinsed and soaked for 1 hour), roughly chopped

1 tablespoon capers (preferably salt-packed, then rinsed and soaked), roughly chopped

1 tablespoon minced fresh sage

2 tablespoons unsalted butter, softened

Salt and freshly ground black pepper

Plenty of crusty baguette slices, for serving

Place a large sauté pan over high heat and add the oil. Add the carrots, onions, and celery, sauté for 1 minute, then turn the heat down to medium-low and cook, stirring occasionally, for about 20 minutes, or until the vegetables are soft.

Meanwhile, roughly chop the chicken livers on a large cutting board (liver is pretty messy, so set your cutting board in a large baking sheet to make cleanup easier).

When the carrots and onions are cooked, increase the heat to high and add the livers. Sauté for 3 to 4 minutes, then reduce the heat to medium and cook for 10 to 15 minutes, stirring frequently, until the livers are cooked through. Add the wine and cook until it is evaporated, 3 to 5 minutes. Add the stock and cook, stirring, until it is evaporated, 3 to 5 minutes. The mixture should be nice and moist but not liquidy. Stir the anchovies and capers into the mixture with the sage and butter. Remove the pan from the heat.

Scoop the liver mixture onto a large, clean cutting board, let cool slightly, and chop finely. Put the mixture in a large bowl, season with salt and pepper, and drizzle with olive oil to taste. Mix well.

Lightly toast the baguette slices.

Drizzle the toasts with olive oil, top with pâté, and serve. Leftovers will keep in the refrigerator in an airtight container for 4 to 5 days.

FLEISHER'S "SECRET" CHICKEN RUB

When Jessica and I first opened the shop, I left it up to her to create a spice rub that would later play a big role in our business; we sell a lot of rotisserie chickens. She read and researched and decided to focus on sage. Sage is a wonderful accompaniment to fatty meats, so it often makes an appearance in sausages and pâtés. It's not a meek herb, announcing itself in everything it touches. So Jess had to find a way to blend it with milder herbs and spices. She wanted to show-case them all but still allow the sage to sing. Our customers always comment on the rub, wanting to know what's in our blend. Now it's no longer our secret. We suggest you also use it on ribs, roasts, chops, and even fish. There's almost nothing that doesn't benefit from a good rub.

❖ **MAKES 2 CUPS**

⅓ cup coarse salt

⅓ cup dried sage

⅓ cup garlic powder

¼ cup onion flakes

¼ cup paprika

3 tablespoons dried thyme

3 tablespoons freshly ground black pepper

3 tablespoons dried oregano

1 tablespoon cayenne

In a large bowl, combine the salt, sage, garlic powder, onion flakes, paprika, thyme, black pepper, oregano, and cayenne. Rub the dried herbs between your palms to crush them as you add each to the mixture. This rub will keep in an airtight container for 6 months. Shake or mix well before using.

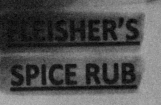

FLEISHER'S
SPICE RUB

- Sea Salt
  Garlic
  Onion
  Black Pepper
  Oregano
  Sage
  Thyme
  Paprika
  Cayenne

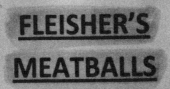

FLEISHER'S
MEATBALLS

Sea Salt
Garlic
Onion
Black Pepper
Oregano
Sage
Parsley

SOURCING

THERE IS A SUSTAINABLE FOOD MOVEMENT AFOOT, and other people are out there doing what we do. We don't ship, because we prefer that people come to see what we're about or support their own local industry and farmers. (Not to mention the fact that the carbon footprint of shipping is monumental, and meat doesn't travel well.) Take the time to find good, local farmers before you shop. *Where* you shop is as important as *what* you shop for. Farmers' markets, Community Supported Agriculture (CSA) meat shares (see page 224), farm stands, direct sale from farms, and natural food stores are far more likely to have good choices than most supermarkets. Some butcher shops stock pastured meat, but most carry the same boxed stuff supermarkets do.

When choosing where to spend your money, it helps to know what you're looking to buy. Everyone has personal must-haves and limitations. I hope we've given you ample information regarding what to consider when buying meat. Some people prefer USDA organic at all costs; others just want to know that the animals were completely free to roam on pasture. Maybe you only want fresh, never frozen, or only regional.

Once you know what you want, you can start asking questions at local markets and stores to find out where it's available. If you are speaking to the actual farmer, inquire about where the animals are kept, how often they're outside, what they were fed, and where they were slaughtered. Ask if you can visit the farm. Ask about hormones and antibiotics, too. As we've mentioned, some small farmers treat sick animals with antibiotics. This is vastly different from feeding them prophylactically to caged animals. If you're joining a pastured meat collective, definitely look into visiting the farm or farms your share will be coming from. You should find animals there. It sounds like a no-brainer, but sometimes people are selling animals they aren't raising. That's not great traceability. Farms shouldn't be too noisy; troubled animals are loud. And they should be relatively clean, but, remember, these are farms—animals aren't pristine.

If you want 100 percent grass-fed beef, make sure to ask how the steers are finished and what they're given to eat in the winter when grass isn't always on the ground. And if sellers are calling their products organic—in markets, butcher shops, stores, wherever—they should be able to show you a certificate to back up that claim. If they are marketing their meat as "natural," ask them what that actually means. Just because something is being sold in a farmers' market or a Whole Foods–type store that doesn't automatically make it pure, and it doesn't mean you shouldn't ask questions. If you buy something—no matter where—get it home, and don't like it, don't give up entirely. Ask more questions at the farmers' market the following week. Call the butcher and explain what you didn't like and how you cooked what you bought. The farmer or the butcher or the shopkeeper should be able to suggest a different cut or cooking method.

If you go to a butcher shop, there should be no bad smell. The shop must be clean and appetizing. The cases should be inviting and full of freshly cut, moist, blood-red meat that is "blooming"— when you cut meat it turns bright red in the presence of oxygen. Dried-out, brown meat with curling edges isn't fresh and is unappetizing at best, dangerous at worst. Even if you hit the shop at a quiet moment, there should still be an engaged, dynamic feel. You want a staff that can answer your questions without arrogance or surliness, and butchers who can tell you where the meat is from and how to cook it. The best places will age their own meat (even if they just age the loins). They'll also make their own sausages, though most shops use commercial spice mixtures and call them homemade—like diners that serve "baked on premises" pies that were actually made somewhere else and delivered to them frozen.

With a CSA-style share, you're buying meat as a member of a collective, so you know more going in about what you will be getting. You aren't blindly approaching a new farmer at a market and attempting to establish trust. You'll be able to read about (or possibly visit) the farm or farms supplying the meat before you join, so all questions you have about feed, treatment, drugs, and slaughter might already have been addressed. Shares tend to be delivered once a month, typically frozen. Some give you whatever they choose to give you; others allow members to order what they want. If you're looking to get hooked up with a meat share, you can research them on websites like localharvest .org (for other resources, see page 233), or ask your CSA vegetable farmer or at your favorite farmers' market stand. If you want something specific that isn't being offered, speak up. Farmers might be more than happy to cut to order. They might not be offering hearts or kidneys because they don't sell overly well in America, but that doesn't mean they won't give you some. One caveat: if the share offers meat from various farms, deliveries might not be consistent in cut and flavor from one to the next. If you have a big family or a group of friends willing to go in on a share, buying a whole, half, or quarter animal from a farmer is another solid way to obtain good pastured meat.

SUPERMARKETS

If farmers' markets, meat shares, and the rest of these options are not for you, and you really just want to be able to go to your supermarket and get some meat that's okay to eat, then familiarize yourself with the labels on pages 226–31 before you shop. Generally speaking, supermarkets are the most overwhelming places to look for sustainable meat. To ferret out what might be good in a sea of mainly bad, you really have to be an educated label reader and a natural-born skeptic. There are so many seemingly acceptable products in these cases, littered with phrases like "natural," "free range," "cage free," and "vegetarian fed"—all carefully constructed to draw in the consumer, even down to the earthy colors of the packaging. It's tricky. These marketing ploys trigger trust in consumers, but most are ultimately bogus, meaningless, and unregulated.

We have put in some serious time reading labels on—and taste testing—supermarket meat. We even take our apprentices on label-reading excursions at a local Wal-Mart. We choose this spot over other nearby supermarkets because it sells the ultimate array of industrialized meat, though it is starting to stock more organic produce. Sometimes we spend three hours straight in there, making our way from the deli counter to the cases of beef, pork, and chicken (almost no lamb is sold) and winding up by the monstrous family packs of hot dogs. This exercise is a reality check. But it's crucial for us to understand—and to train the next wave of butchers to understand—what and how most Americans eat. Wal-Mart's football field–sized meat section is much more familiar to most people than our checkerboard floors and lovingly arranged cases. Something as seemingly simple as a quarter pound of sliced ham is perfect in its ability to illustrate the issues of factory-farming methodology and the uses of nitrates/nitrites, coloring, fillers, and flavoring agents.

As you stand in front of a supermarket case, don't be swayed by color. Many supermarkets and processing houses pump carbon monoxide into the packaging, a deceptive technique that keeps meat red and fresh-looking even when it's weeks old. Instead, start reading. The claims found on packages of meat mean different things and some are far more regulated than others.

Most packaged supermarket meat is filled with water and additives to make it moist and "flavorful." In his book *Kitchen Pro Series: Guide to Meat Identification, Fabrication, and Utilization*, Tom Schneller says additives include "water flavor, water retention agent, isolated soy protein, moistness solutions, moisture and flavor agent." We really couldn't even begin to imagine what "water flavor" is, or tell you if that isolated soy is genetically modified or not, but it's certainly not meat. In fact, 15 percent of most packaged meat is not meat. By law these products must be labeled with an "ingredient" list.

That said, there is a sliding scale here—the boxed stuff that is actually raised on family farms and largely devoid of drugs is a better choice than a factory-farm version. Unfortunately it is hard to know what "better" really is and how much you can trust it. If you aren't finding enough—or any—better choices at your supermarket, speak up. Ask the management for what you want and leave comments in the comments box. Get your friends, neighbors, and any groups you belong to to do the same. The more people who demand better meat, the more likely the store is to stock it. If you won't buy it, it won't come.

FREEZER ORDERS

Buying a quarter, a side, or a whole animal from a farmer is one of the best ways to purchase sustainably raised pastured meat. It gives you the opportunity to check out the farm and order exactly what you want, but there are a number of things to keep in mind when you do this. Follow these guidelines for beef for the best results. Be cautious if the farmer/butcher or processor is unwilling to work within your specifications. Lambs and pigs have a similar set of parameters, but each animal has its own intricacies. A good butcher should be able to guide you through this process with ease.

When you order is just as important as what you order. If you place your order in September you should ask for lots of roasts, stew meat, and other braising goodies. Also keep in mind that big holidays like Christmas, New Year's, and Passover/Easter are coming up, so you may want to request larger, fancier roasts like prime rib or tenderloin for those occasions.

Regardless of the season, always take into account how you cook—are you a griller or a Crock-Potter?—and how big your family is. If you have a family of four or more, you may want to have more roasts than stew or grind so that you can send the kids to school with sandwiches and take some for your own lunch the next day.

To give you an idea of what and how to order, we have broken down a freezer order for a split side of beef (a split side is half of a side). We suggest that you share a side with friends or family and have that divided into split sides. This works especially well for families with small children because it will not overwhelm you and is extremely economical, and you should run through the meat in your freezer within four to six months (well before freezer burn starts to set in). A side, which should last six to eight months, is great for a family with growing boys or many kids. Always reorder *before* you run out, as sometimes it takes a while for the farmer/slaughterhouse to be able to connect and process your meat.

A split side of an 800-pound beef carcass will contain:

2 bone-out and chuck eye roasts, each weighing 3 pounds
1 shoulder clod roast, 3 pounds
7 rib steaks, each 1 inch thick
2 T-bone steaks, each 1 inch thick
5 porterhouse steaks, each 1 inch thick
3 to 4 sirloin steaks, each 1 inch thick
Top round/3 London broils, each 1½ inches thick

Bottom round roast, 4 pounds
½ eye round roast, 2 to 2½ pounds
Sirloin tip roast, 4 to 5 pounds
Brisket, 2 to 2½ pounds
Stew meat, 4 to 5 pounds
Ground meat, 80/20 fat-to-lean mixture, 25 to 30 pounds

QUESTIONS TO CONSIDER

❖ Will this order be paper-wrapped or vacuum-sealed? You may have to pay an additional fee for vacuum sealing. (See our freezer recommendations for both on page 97.)

❖ How thick do you want your steak to be? If you are splitting an order with a friend, make sure he or she agrees—you can't split a side and order two different thicknesses. The standard is ¾ inch, but we feel that is too thin; the thinnest steak we would recommend is a 1-inch cut. Bone-in or bone-out is another decision to consider. Always make sure you decide how many steaks you want per package.

❖ How much do you want your roasts to weigh? The standard is 3 to 4 pounds, but that size will give lots of leftovers for a family of four. You may want to downsize or upgrade to larger sizes for parties.

❖ Do you want your ground meat to be the standard (and our recommended mixture—see page 162) 80/20 blend or a leaner grind? And decide how much ground you want per package; we suggest ½ pound per person, so for a family of four a 2-pound package is perfect.

❖ Can your processor make your ground meat into 4- or 8-ounce patties? (There may be an additional charge for patties.)

❖ Do you want the skirt or flank? If yes, speak up because there is only one per side and most often it is thrown into the "grind" pile. Any item you don't mention will end up as ground or stew meat.

❖ Do you want fatty or lean stew meat? How many pounds per package?

❖ Do you want the sirloin flap cut into steaks or stir-fry strips? (Some processors do not offer this option.)

❖ Do you expect to receive a hanger? The "butcher's tender" needs to be pulled immediately after an animal is slaughtered and not aged. Most places won't take it off and hold it for you. This, of course, only pertains to whole animal orders.

❖ Do you want bones? Should they be cut for soup? Do you want marrow bones?

❖ Do you want short ribs? If yes, how do you want them cut?

❖ Do you want the heart, liver, tongue, or tail?

LABEL READING 101

The following labels and terms can be useful to consumers in search of better meat. I wish I could tell you that they are easy to understand. They're not. Even the good ones are full of loopholes, and the definitions are questioned, petitioned against by various groups, and changed frequently. It's a full-time job to stay on top of them. Here is our take on what they mean, generally speaking, and how trustworthy we find them to be. Always look for a label that requires third-party certification—meaning that an unbiased party has verified that the claims and standards the label represents are actually being met. Ultimately we believe a safer way to go is to know and trust your local farmer or butcher. As with all things in life, there's no such thing as 100 percent clarity.

Phrases That Make Us Suspicious

The following labels should mean a lot, but in the absence of third-party certification they tend to mean very little or nothing at all, unless you know and trust the producer. There seems to be consumer confusion over the fact that although many of these labels are *defined* by the USDA, they aren't *verified* by the USDA (or a third party). Except for the few labels that require third-party certification to back up the claim, it's basically up to the industry to self-police. This can lead to labels getting used where they don't actually apply because producers can get more money for products that are stamped with these words. Regulation is rare.

NATURAL The word *natural* on most food products is a marketing sham. We do not use the terms *natural* or *all-natural* in the shop. In 2009 the USDA (re)defined the term *naturally raised* specifically for meat, in an effort to clear up some of the confusion surrounding the widely used claim. Its definition is as follows:

> Livestock used for the production of meat and meat products that have been raised entirely without growth promotants, antibiotics (except for ionophores used as coccidiostats for parasite control), and have never been fed animal (mammalian, avian, or aquatic) by-products derived from the slaughter/harvest processes, including meat and fat, animal waste materials (e.g., manure and litter), and aquatic by-products (e.g., fishmeal and fish oil). . . . If ionophores used only to prevent parasitism were administered to the animals, they may be labeled with the naturally raised marketing claims if that fact is explicitly noted.

If you didn't just slip into a coma reading that, then you might realize that this explanation doesn't even hint at how the animals are raised. So, obviously, this term doesn't go quite far enough for us, especially as no third-party certification is required; therefore, it's unregulated. If a producer is truly following USDA standards, the resulting meat is clearly a better choice than conventional but nowhere near as good as well-raised local pastured or USDA organic. *Natural,* on the other hand, means only that the meat has not had anything added to it, like dyes, brines, salt, or flavorings and is unregulated.

NO HORMONES ADMINISTERED It isn't legal to give hogs and poultry hormones, so if you see this phrase on pork or chicken, it's pure marketing. Hormones are permitted for use in ruminants in the United States; however, this claim isn't third-party certified. Even if a package of meat is marked free of growth hormones, keep reading for a label like USDA Organic or Certified Humane, which would back up that claim. Or talk to your farmers or purveyors to see how they trace their animals from birth to slaughter.

NO ANTIBIOTICS ADMINISTERED This claim *should* mean that no antibiotics were given to an animal during its lifetime, but it isn't third-party certified, and animals are not being routinely tested for antibiotics. Even if they were, some farmers try to get around this by taking their animals off antibiotics for two weeks prior to slaughter to remove traces of the drugs from the bloodstream. But anyone

who watches sports knows traces of drugs remain in the muscle and hair follicles for months and even years. In the absence of another label from a trustworthy certifying agency, this claim, like "no hormones administered," isn't reliable unless you know and trust your farmers or purveyors and how they work.

100 PERCENT VEGETARIAN FEED This label signifies that animals aren't fed any animal by-products, but it doesn't cover anything beyond that (drugs, for example). Once again, it is not third-party certified. And it doesn't actually mean that the animals were raised on pasture. Consumers interested in a 100 percent grass-fed product should understand that "vegetarian" includes grains. Sometimes you see *no animal by-products* instead. This is also unverified.

FREE-RANGE/FREE-ROAMING *Free-range* or *free-roaming* implies that the animal had some access to the outdoors, possibly just a tiny pen, but this USDA-defined term doesn't guarantee that any time was actually spent outside. To further confuse you, the USDA has defined this term for poultry (remember: defining something is not the same thing as certifying it) but not for eggs. So if you see "free-range" on eggs it doesn't mean anything. We prefer the term *pastured,* but recognize this also isn't third-party certified. Still, you mainly see pastured eggs in a farmers' market, and there you can talk to the farmer about what it means and decide for yourself if you're comfortable with the response. Remember, *free-range* signifies nothing about drugs or feed.

CAGE-FREE Just because a bird isn't in a cage doesn't mean it's outside. It can still be stuck in an overcrowded barn, just not in a cage in an overcrowded barn. Again, we prefer "pastured" eggs.

Trust These Terms If You Know Your Producer

GRASS-FED OR 100 PERCENT GRASS-FED We use this term a lot, and we have our own definition of it. To us, *grass-fed* means ruminants raised exclusively (i.e., 100 percent) on grass and dried stored grasses. Diet supplements must be grain-free and contain no animal products. There's a government-defined version, too, and some people in our sustainable food circles lament that it has a loophole for confinement and feedlots. Third-party certification is not required. The label *grass-fed/grain-finished* is equally unregulated. The grain is usually corn. These claims tend to be used to refer to animals raised on small family farms. You must know your farmers—or the people who sell their meat—to ensure they are producing truly "grass-fed" animals.

LOCAL Locavores like to quote the following statistic: refrigerating, transporting, and storing food requires eight times as much energy than is provided by the food itself in calories. Also, whenever food leaves the community in which it was produced, money leaves with it. By buying local you are supporting family farms and small businesses. But what the label *local* indicates is pretty wide-ranging and entirely unregulated. For us, it means within a three-hour radius, by car, from the shop. If you see the term when shopping, ask questions to find out what it signifies for others.

PASTURED/PASTURE-RAISED/FREE-FARMED None of these terms are USDA defined and are therefore pretty meaningless unless you know the producer. At Fleisher's, *pastured* means plenty. We use this term for our pigs, steers, and lambs—they always have access to pasture and can be fed grain if that is the way the farmer chooses to raise them—and for veal (when we have it) to give it absolute distinction from conventional veal reared in pens separated from their mothers. Ask your butcher, farmer, or shopkeeper what he or she means by these terms if you see them on a package or at a meat counter.

SUSTAINABLE Once again, while this is a widely used term in farmers' market circles, it has no legal meaning. In order to know what is meant by it, and if you can trust it, you must know your producers. It is used to refer to food that sustains the planet by not harming it via pollution or overuse of resources like water. It also sustains producers, by providing them a solid consistent wage and a healthy environment to work in, and eaters, by being pure and nutritious. Sustainably raised animals should be treated humanely.

Third-Party-Certified Labels to Rely on (Especially When at a Supermarket)

USDA CERTIFIED ORGANIC As described on page 38, in order to be labeled *organic,* a product, its producer, and the farm where the ingredients come from must meet the USDA's organic standards and must be third-party certified by a USDA-approved food-certifying agency. Synthetic fertilizers, chemicals, sewage sludge, genetic modification, and irradiation are banned. However, contrary to what most people believe, organic does not automatically mean pesticide-free. It means that pesticides, if used, must be derived from natural sources, not synthetically manufactured. Even natural pesticides can be harmful (they are designed to kill things, after all). Most organic farmers (and even some conventional farmers) employ additional methods to help control pests, including insect traps, careful crop selection (there are disease-resistant varieties),

Some large companies do offer a more "natural" product than traditional factory farms. They usually have a number of contract farmers growing their animals for them. If you see a package of meat claiming to be naturally raised, look for trustworthy certifications that back up this claim, like "Certified Humane" or "AWA Approved." Without them, it's anyone's guess whether these animals are actually raised without drugs and on good, safe feed. But if the choice is natural or conventional, we would go with natural every time!

and biological controls (such as predator insects and beneficial microorganisms).

Organic meat and poultry must be fed only organically grown feed (without any animal by-products) and cannot be treated with hormones or antibiotics. Animals must have access to the outdoors, and ruminants must have access to pasture (but don't actually have to go outdoors and graze on pasture to be considered organic). Keep an eye out for "100 percent organic" as opposed to just "organic" (this is only at least 95 percent organic) or "made with organic ingredients" (this is only at least 70 percent organic). Not enough consumers know that it's not all 100 percent. The USDA National Organic Program maintains a list of what nonorganic items are allowed in that 5 percent or 30 percent. If you are interested, you can look through lists of these items, as well as what is exempt from having to be organic in a fully organic product, at ams.usda.gov.

ANIMAL WELFARE APPROVED (AWA) This nonprofit annually audits the family farms using its logo and only grants use—at no charge—to those complying with progressive and humane animal welfare standards spanning birth to death. Animals must be on pasture. We like AWA and think they're doing amazing things, but we acknowledge that their standards don't always make the most sense for all farmers.

CERTIFIED HUMANE RAISED AND HANDLED This is a fairly meaningful third-party-certified label that indicates meat, dairy, and eggs come from animals that were treated humanely. It's also nonprofit, but bigger than AWA. Growth hormones and antibiotics in feed are prohibited. There are strict guidelines for slaughter. Some critics quibble that this certification is awarded to farms that are too big, or too industrial. Still, if your choice is between something conventional and something conventional that has earned this label, grab the latter.

BIODYNAMIC Biodynamic farmers follow practices similar to those outlined by organic standards—and often go beyond those. Livestock must be pastured and vegetables are planted in accordance with cycles of the moon. There is one certification agency in the United States: Demeter USA.

ANIMAL PRODUCTS

Dairy and eggs should also be carefully chosen. If you have a source for good meat, they should be able to point you in the direction of equally good milk, cheese, butter, yogurt, ice cream, and eggs—or sell these products themselves. We do. Before you shop for dairy and eggs, decide what you are looking for, as you did with meat. Only you can make those decisions. The milk we sell in the store isn't organic, but it is local and we personally know and trust the guys. We also love that it comes in reusable glass bottles. The cows are raised on a diet of grass and grain, and aren't given hormones or prophylactic antibiotics. If you

WHAT TO LOOK FOR IN EGGS

❖ Hard shells, bright orange yolks, thick whites. These specimens are best found at farmers' markets, farm stands, and CSAs.

❖ Most supermarket eggs are at least two to three months old; eggs sold at farmers' markets tend to be far younger and may even be freshly laid.

❖ If you're unclear about the age of your egg, pop it in water: if it floats, it's old. If it is fresh, it sinks.

❖ When you're buying eggs at a store, read all labels and look for the trustworthy ones. Don't be tricked by contrived farm names and do read all fine print. We have seen "Hudson Valley Farm" eggs on our Wal-Mart excursions that we'd discovered, on further carton reading, were actually packed far away in Arkansas.

want organic milk from cows that are 100 percent grass-fed, seek that out. Understand that not all dairies—even certified organic ones—are created equal. There are giant organic dairies that are pretty similar to conventional ones—minus the feed and lack of drugs administered. When choosing milk, you can also seek out all levels of pasteurization—raw (which is illegal in many states), low or lightly, or ultra. If you don't buy organic, keep an eye out for "rBGH-free." This hormone, used to stimulate lactation in cows, has been linked to cancers and is banned in many places around the world, including the European Union, Canada, Japan, and Australia. Though rBGH-free isn't a third-party-certified claim, it's still something to look for. When it comes to cheeses, sourcing local ones cannot be considered a hardship. You basically have to seek out ones that are made from good milk, then taste everything and decide what you like. Tough job, but someone has to do it.

RESOURCES

We know how hard it is to understand the issues surrounding well-raised meat. The websites, books, and shops that follow can help.

WEBSITES

❖ The Cornucopia Institute, a nonprofit organic watchdog group, maintains an information-filled website. Check out their organic dairy report and scorecard at cornucopia.org.

❖ For locating everything from farm shares to natural food markets, go to localharvest.org; ams.usda.gov/amsv1.0/farmersmarkets; and nal.usda.gov/afsic/pubs/csa/csa.shtml.

❖ For everything you ever wanted to know about grass feeding, plus shopping resources, the site to head to is eatwild.com.

❖The American Pastured Poultry Producers Association lists producers by state and other consumer-friendly details at apppa.org.

❖ To learn more about how to read labels, check out greenerchoices.org and eatwellguide.org.

❖ Food safety information, government-style, is at foodsafety.nal.usda.gov.

❖ Most states have good cheese sites; search online for yours. We have bookmarked nyfarmcheese.org.

❖ The official site for USDA organic is ams.usda.gov/nop.

❖ For the nongovernment consumer watchdog take on all things organic, go to organicconsumers.org.

❖ The websites for both bovine and porcine myology are incredible resources for seeing a carcass from the inside out: bovine.unl.edu/bovine3D/eng/rota.jsp and porcine.unl.edu/porcine2005/pages/index.jsp.

❖ Texas A&M University has an excellent meat science program and offers a three-day Beef 101 class. Check it out at animalscience.tamu.edu/academics/meat-science/workshops.

❖ Iowa State University has a respected meat science program, which also offers short courses on curing and drying sausages. Read about it at ans.iastate.edu.

❖ We love grist.org and get a lot of our sustainable food news from here. We especially enjoy Tom Philpott's incisive essays on the meat industry.

❖ One of our odd little hobbies is checking on the revoked statuses listed on the CCOF Organic Certification Association website, ccof.org/no_longer_cert.php.

❖ Temple Grandin has a website, grandin.com. Read it.

❖ See which farms are Animal Welfare Approved at animalwelfareapproved.org.

❖ *Righteous Porkchop* by Nicolette Hahn Niman is one of our book suggestions. It's also a blog: righteousporkchop.com/righteousblog.

❖ The Livable Future blog has great information on antibiotics, drug resistance, and factory farming: livablefutureblog.com.

❖ If you are all riled up about what's on your plate, civileats.com is a great place to get politically aware and involved.

❖ Foodandwaterwatch.org is another good place to take action.

❖ The National Family Farm Coalition maintains a great site for finding out about the issues that threaten family farms in this country: nffc.net/index.html.

❖ The Institute for Agriculture and Trade Policy offers a more global perspective on sustainability, food politics, and climate change: iatp.org.

❖ Sustainable Table is one of our very favorite websites for facts, figures, places to shop and eat, and ideas on how to live a sustainable life: sustainabletable.org.

❖ The Ethicurean is a great site for sustainable foodie news and has good book reviews: ethicurian.com.

❖ The Glynwood Institute for Sustainable Food and Farming has information on the mobile slaughterhouse initiative and other critical issues: glynwood.org.

❖ The Grace Foundation's (those fine folks who have given us the Sustainable Table and Eat Well Guide websites as well as the Meatrix) blog is at ecocentricblog.org.

❖ Good, geeky info on food, agriculture, and energy can be found at the Union of Concerned Scientists' site: ucsusa.org.

❖ The Meatrix—we insist that everyone we know sees these funny yet terrifying cartoons: themeatrix.com.

❖ Food Democracy Now is another place to vote with your fork: fooddemocracynow.org.

❖ The Humane Society website has great information on farm animal cruelty and CAFOs. It's a little too vegan for our tastes but contains solid information brought to you by people who have made it their livelihood to care: humanesociety.org/issues/eating.

❖ Food Animal Concerns is another group focused on farm animals. They've got excellent articles on filthy feed at foodanimalconcerns.org.

❖ Pew Charitable Trusts Human Health and Industrial Farming Campaign specializes in all things concerning antibiotics and industrial farming. Their fascinating reports are at saveantibiotics.org.

❖ We are such big fans we actually look forward to Food Safety News's daily (and horrifying) e-blasts. Sign up at foodsafetynews.com.

❖ The grande dame of food politics, author and professor Marion Nestle, is an inspiration and a powerhouse. Read what she's thinking about at foodpolitics.com.

❖ Take a walk on the other side and read the *Business Journal for Meat and Poultry Processors* at meatpoultry.com.

❖ The Meating Place is an online community for meat processing and poultry processors. Join the fun at meatingplace.com.

BOOKS

Animals in Translation: Using the Mysteries of Autism to Decode Animal Behavior by Temple Grandin

The CAFO Reader: The Tragedy of Industrial Animal Factories by Daniel Imhoff

Charcuterie: The Craft of Salting, Smoking, and Curing by Michael Ruhlman and Brian Polcyn

Cleaving: A Story of Marriage, Meat, and Obsession by Julie Powell

The Conscious Kitchen: The New Way to Buy and Cook Food—To Protect the Earth, Improve Your Health, and Eat Deliciously by Alexandra Zissu

Fast Food Nation: The Dark Side of the All-American Meal by Eric Schlosser

The Flavor Bible: The Essential Guide to Culinary Creativity, Based on the Wisdom of America's Most Imaginative Chefs by Karen Page and Andrew Dornenburg

Heat: An Amateur's Adventures as Kitchen Slave, Line Cook, Pasta-Maker, and Apprentice to a Dante-Quoting Butcher in Tuscany by Bill Buford

The Jungle by Upton Sinclair

Kitchen Pro Series: Guide to Meat Identification, Fabrication, and Utilization and *Guide to Poultry Identification, Fabrication, and Utilization* by Thomas Schneller and the Culinary Institute of America

Meat: A Kitchen Education by James Peterson

The Meat Buyer's Guide and *The Poultry Buyer's Guide* by the North American Meat Processors Association

The Niman Ranch Cookbook: From Farm to Table with America's Finest Meat by Bill Niman and Janet Fletcher

The Omnivore's Dilemma: A Natural History of Four Meals by Michael Pollan

Pig Perfect: Encounters with Remarkable Swine and Some Great Ways to Cook Them by Peter Kaminsky

Pork and Sons by Stéphane Reynaud

Primal Cuts: Cooking with America's Best Butchers by Marissa Guggiana

Raising Steaks: The Life and Times of American Beef by Betty Fussell

Righteous Porkchop: Finding a Life and Good Food Beyond Factory Farms by Nicolette Hahn Niman

The River Cottage Meat Book by Hugh Fearnley-Whittingstall

Salad Bar Beef and *Everything I Want to Do Is Illegal* by Joel Salatin

Seven Fires: Grilling the Argentine Way by Francis Mallmann and Peter Kaminsky

The Whole Beast: Nose to Tail Eating by Fergus Henderson

SOURCES

❖ The herbs and spices for our rubs, sausages, and marinades come from Mountain Rose Herbs: mountainroseherbs.com.

❖ For all of your butcher paper, twine, cutting, and sausage-making needs, head to butcher-packer.com or sausagemaker.com.

❖ For our favorite stovetop-to-oven steel pans, check out www.debuyer.com.

❖ For our preferred enamel-coated cast-iron pots, visit lecreuset.com.

❖ For more specifics on roasting whole pigs, including charcoal, wood, building fires, tips, and timing as you plan your roast, go to the sections on roasting a whole pig at firepit-and-grilling-guru.com and askthemeatman.com.

❖ The all important metal aprons can be found at Saf-T-Guard, saftguard.com.

ACKNOWLEDGMENTS

Josh and Jessica Applestone would like to thank the "old men" of the business who taught us everything we know: Tom, Bob, Kent, Bill, Jan, Hans, and of course, Ted. Special thanks to Mike Meiller; your skills and facilities are exceptional. You make what we do possible. All the farmers we have ever worked with, especially Stephen Kaye, who showed us what grass-fed was all about, and David Huse, who made it even better. Thanks to Richard and his boys at Hilltown Pork. The chefs, restaurateurs, and their staffs that have supported us all these years as well as Peter Hoffman, Dan Barber, Adam Kaye, Donna Lennard, and Ed Witt, who believed in us from the beginning and have given energy to the movement. Spencer Mass and the Country Inn family, who have always provided us with moments of sanity and good food. Caroline Fidenza, who saw potential in a "crazy" idea and made it work. And Steve Slutzky, our smoking buddy. Our customers, we would be nothing without you. We are so blessed that so many of you have been with us since day one. Our employees both past and present, we could not be what we are without you. Our apprentices for carrying on the tradition, and especially Bryan Mayer, who has become a trusted employee and a deeply valued friend. The boys at the Meat Hook, especially Tom Mylan, you make us proud, bubbie! Our investors for believing in us, you truly are angels. Joe Concra and Denise Orzo for being the best welcome wagon ever. Dana Bowen for making our parents "kvell" for the first time. Julie Powell, for embodying the truest essence of a *bouchère*—tough, generous, and loyal. Jen May, our friend, and resident staff photographer, for making what we see as beautiful actually beautiful. Gunar Skillins, how fortuitous it was that one of the best (and most patient) graphic designers wandered into our shop one day. Kendra McKnight, food stylist, for helping to make our food as pretty as it is tasty. Liv Grey for her patience, professionalism, and precision—everything a recipe tester should be. And Dietrich Gehring. Stacy Strauss and Craig McCord, who feed our vision. David Nelson, the definition of a mensch. Suzanne Wasserman for your historical illumination on butchery, New York, and all those good things. Richard "Peachpits" Frumess—a master of the written word. Our landlord, Carter Hastings, for giving us a chance. Stephen Gates, for being a friend, confidant, and adviser. Matt Unger, Stephanie Ehrlich, and Jordan Berkowitz, who have known us since the beginning, touched our hearts, made us laugh, and have indelibly left your marks on our business. Juan Pablo Lopez, with us from the beginning, we never forget that you are our rock—we literally could not have done it without you. Aaron "Chocolate Thunder" Lenz, Hailey "Schmailey" Pearson, Erica Murray, Josh "BJ" Graves—you have become family. Our friends and family who have stood by us and sometimes behind us propping us up during hard times. We couldn't live without you. Lexy, whose patience, stamina, and humor have made this project a pleasure, and for making our voices and philosophy tangible and accessible—beautifully. Olli "Tube Steak" Chanoff for supporting Lexy and by extension us; this project was made possible by you as well. Samantha Gloeffke for taking care of Izzy with grace and humor and in turn taking care of us. Each other, for never giving up, and our son, Isaiah Wolf, for keeping us sane.

Alexandra Zissu thanks Jess and Josh for opening Fleisher's and providing me, my family, and countless others access to small amounts of consistently flavorful, meticulously sourced, well-raised meat; for taking me up on my offer to write their story; for bringing me further along on my quest to truly know where my food comes from; and for turning up the volume on the conversation about sustainable meat. Bottomless gratitude also goes to my lovely family, especially Olli Chanoff, Aili Chanoff Zissu, my multitasking and supportive parents—Zissus and Meaders alike (and the Van Steenburgh homestead!), and the beyond helpful Chanoff clan. Thanks also to dear friends who, when I went MIA for most of 2010, ordered Fleisher's home delivery to taste what I was up to or froze in a field to witness a slaughter. I owe you dinner and you know what I'm making.

The three of us could never have produced these pages without and are very grateful to Rica Allannic, Amy Hughes, Marysarah Quinn, Ashley Phillips, Christine Tanigawa, Alexis Mentor, Lauren Shakely, Doris Cooper, Allison Malec, Jacob Bronstein, Jill Browning, Kate Tyler, and Donna Passannante.

INDEX